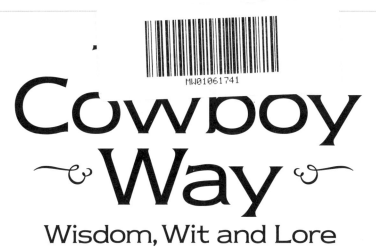

Cowboy
~&~ Way ~&~

Wisdom, Wit and Lore

Duane S. Radford

BLUE
BIKE
BOOKS

The Publisher: Blue Bike Books

Website: www.bluebikebooks.com

Library and Archives Canada Cataloguing in Publication

Radford, Duane S., 1946–, author
The cowboy way : wisdom, wit and lore / Duane S. Radford.

Includes bibliographical references.
ISBN 978-1-926700-46-5 (pbk.)

1. Cowboys—United States—Miscellanea. 2. Cowboys—Canada—Miscellanea.
I. Title.

F596.R33 2014   636.2'130971   C2014-900023-5

Project Director: Nicholle Carrière
Project Editor: Nicholle Carrière
Map: Volker Bodegom
Front and Back Cover Images: front cover photo © Troy Boman / Photos.com; back cover photo © John Pitcher / Photos.com; back cover leather labels © Leysan / Thinkstock
Photo credits: Every effort has been made to accurately credit the sources of photographs. Please inform the publisher of any errors or omissions. Ron Adair, 23; AigarsR / Photos.com, 238; Androsov / Photos.com, 80; Bain News Service / Library of Congress, 219; D.F. Barry / Library of Congress, 212; Deborah Cheramie / Photos.com, 108; Giles Coudert / Wikipedia, 92; Fort Whoop-Up Interpretive Society, 134; R.K. Fox / Library of Congress, 213; Glenbow Archives, 28, 44, 58, 59, 62, 71; John C.H. Grabill / Library of Congress, 90; Grombo / Wikipedia, 86; International Communications Systems, 248; Maria Itina / Photos.com, 113; Dean Jarvey / Wikipedia, 198; Lauren Johnson / Photos.com, 109; Jupiterimages / Photos.com, 127, 131, 204, 208; Robert Koopmans / Photos.com, 82; Holly Kuchera / Photos.com, 172; Russell Lee / Library of Congress, 27, 37, 94, 97; Library of Congress, 19, 73, 126, 139, 148, 150, 153, 185, 195; Lithistman / Wikipedia, 87; Erik Lizee / Wikipedia, 30; Robyn MacKenzie / Photos.com, 107; Larry D. Moore / Wikipedia, 91, 272; Jim Parkin / Photos.com, 177; Duane Radford, 12, 40, 43, 120, 152, 155, 157, 159, 161, 166, 169, 253; Duane Radford / Travel Alberta, 123, 129; Arthur Rothstein / Library of Congress, 15; sfmorris / Photos.com, 267; Smithsonian Institution, 183; Thinkstock / Photos.com, 115, 124, 191, 259, 261, 264; University of Pennsylvania Archives, 270; Wikipedia, 70, 147; William Henry Jackson / Library of Congress, 26, 99

Produced with the assistance of the Government of Alberta

We acknowledge the financial support of the Government of Canada.
Nous reconnaissons l'appui financier du gouvernement du Canada.

Funded by the Government of Canada   Financé par le gouvernement du Canada | Canadä

PC: 38-2

DEDICATION

This book is dedicated to all the cowboys and their families in Canada and the United States, past and present, in recognition of their immeasurable contributions to North American society. When all is said and done, it was the man on horseback who made the West, and cowboys played an integral role in this regard.

CONTENTS

ACKNOWLEDGMENTS

I'd like to thank Nicholle Carrière, Blue Bike Books publisher, for the opportunity to write this book, for editing the manuscript and for her many valuable contributions. Every writer needs a good editor, and Nicholle has helped me immeasurably in this regard. I can't say how much I appreciate her many helpful suggestions and her creativity.

I'd also like to thank Cindy Pereira, intern, for her help promoting the book, and Aalyssa Atley, marketing and administrative assistant, for photo selection support.

Thanks to Christie Goss, Travel Alberta Team Member, Team Coordinator, Media and Communications, Travel Alberta; Rachelle Colthorp, Regional Media Relations Representative, Kootenay Rockies Tourism; Monica Dickinson, Manager–Communications, Tourism Kamloops; and Daryl Demoskoff, Media Relations Consultant, Tourism Saskatchewan, for providing information regarding cowboys in Alberta, British Columbia and Saskatchewan, respectively, and for sourcing key reference material.

I want to thank Lillian Chan, Program Coordinator, Ag-Industry Extension and Training Branch, Alberta Agriculture, Food and Rural Development, for explaining background related to Alberta's Century Farm and Ranch Award recipients.

I'd also like to thank Chad MacPherson, General Manager, Saskatchewan Stock Growers Association, for providing key historical information about ranches, ranching and pioneer ranchers in Saskatchewan.

Thank you to my sister-in-law Lucille Humble, a music teacher, for checking my text for accuracy with regard to the chapters on cowboy songs and country and western dance.

Many thanks go to John Gattey and Cindy Shipton (Cross Bar Ranch) and Frank and Donna Murphy (Murphy Ranch) in Alberta's Special Areas, for sharing information about ranching and the ranch lifestyle over the years and for their unfailing western hospitality.

I'd be remiss if I didn't acknowledge Rob Tanner, publisher of *Canadian Cowboy Country* magazine, former editors Garry Cooper and Nancy Critchley and current editor Terri Mason for giving me writing assignments about cowboys, western art and artists and western living, and for editing these articles since 2003.

INTRODUCTION

The "Why" of a Book on the Cowboy Way

This particular book is not about fictional cowboys, rather it's a tribute to cowboys who have captured our imagination and personified what we think about the Wild West of bygone days. There are cowboy novels, cowboy movies, cowboy songs and cowboy heroes. There've been cowboy TV series and legendary gunfighters, as well as television and western movies starring actors such as Roy Rogers and his wife, Dale Evans. Cowboys have helped spawn a unique culture and have imparted their trademark humor to folks throughout the world. I've had a long-standing interest in cowboys, having grown up on the edge of ranching country in southwestern Alberta.

As a kid, I worked for several ranchers near the Crowsnest Pass, building fences, stacking hay and doing other chores. Some of my relatives (the Sapeta family, who emigrated from Poland) ranched in the foothills just east of the Livingstone Range, north of Cowley, Alberta, where they homesteaded in the early 1900s. I have vivid memories of my visits to their farms as a child and couldn't help but be impressed with their lifestyle and the many hardships they faced, without complaint. Probably like every little boy in town, I grew up with a six-shooter cap gun and played "Cowboys and Indians" with my friends.

When I worked as a regional director for Alberta's Fish and Wildlife Division, I had a lot of interaction with farmers and ranchers, whom I admired for their work to conserve fish and wildlife resources, and their love of native landscapes. I'm a lifelong outdoorsman, and I continue to hunt

and fish on Alberta's ranchlands to this day. I've been able
to stay in contact with many ranchers from across Alberta
and stay abreast of their issues and concerns. They've
taught me many lessons, one of which is that a hard day's
work won't kill you. As an author, I've written articles for
Canadian Cowboy Country magazine about cowboys, cowboy artists, trail rides and ranches and storied homes in
Alberta and Saskatchewan. I've also done research about
cowboys for Cowboy Country Television. I co-authored
a book, *Conservation Pride and Passion: The Alberta Fish and
Game Association* (2008), with my old buddy, Don Meredith,
for the Alberta Fish and Game Association to celebrate their
history from 1908 to 2008. Many members of this organization are avid outdoorsmen and women; much of the history
of this organization has very close ties with Alberta's farming
and ranching community.

Horses in the Family

My wife, Adrienne, has always enjoyed riding horses and
has spent many days on the trail with her dear friend, Vera
Denecky, who lives in Lethbridge, Alberta. Vera boarded
our daughter Jennifer's horse, Skylark, for many years while
Jennifer was a member of the local 4-H Light Horse Club.
I can remember many of the trials and tribulations of raising
a horse and the challenges that our family faced during these
times. I'm certain that Jennifer's days with 4-H forged her
ability to become a partner in a national law firm in Ottawa.
My son, Myles, on the other hand had a love-hate relationship with horses and probably doesn't have a lot of fond
memories of them. Adrienne and I enjoyed some of the best
days of our lives on trail rides in the magnificent Alberta
Rockies and on trips with Ed Walker in the Ya Ha Tinda,
Brewster Mountain Pack Trains, Holiday on Horseback and
the Trail Riders of the Canadian Rockies. It was on these

trail rides in Alberta's mountains and foothills that I developed a real appreciation for the savvy of horses and their strength and endurance.

If you hang around cowboys, ranchers, trail riders, wranglers and the like, some of their values and beliefs will rub off on you. This association will make you a better person. You'll develop an appreciation for horses and the cowboy lifestyle. You'll probably become a better rider. You'll also develop an appreciation for the magnificence of horses and their strength, abilities and immeasurable importance to cowboys, as well as a healthy respect for horses and how important it is to ensure that a horse understands just who the boss is.

–Duane S. Radford

WHAT IS A COWBOY?

The Vaquero Tradition

The word "cowboy" has its roots in the Spanish word *vaquero*. A vaquero is a horse-mounted livestock herder from a tradition that originated on the Iberian Peninsula in Spain. In modern times, the vaquero is still a part of the Spanish legacy of working, riding horsemanship. The vaquero traditions that developed in Mexico from methodology brought to Mesoamerica from Spain became the foundation for the North American cowboy. The vaqueros of the Americas were the horsemen and cattle herders of Spanish Mexico, who first came to California with the Jesuit priest Eusebio Kino in 1687, and later with expeditions in 1769 and the Juan Bautista de Anza expedition in 1774. They were the first cowboys in the American Southwest.

Natural Horsemanship

In the contemporary United States and Canada, remnants of two major and distinct vaquero traditions remain, known today as the "Texas" tradition and the "Spanish," "Vaquero" or "California" tradition. The popular "horse-whisperer" style of natural horsemanship was originally developed by practitioners who were predominantly from California and the northwestern states, and combined the attitudes and philosophy of the California vaquero with the gear and outward look of the Texas cowboy. The natural horsemanship movement apparently acknowledges that it owes much to the influence of the vaquero tradition.

THE NORTH AMERICAN COWBOY

Justin Gattey of the Cross Bar Ranch, Alberta

Wise Words

The cowboy is a herder, a wrangler, a bronc buster, a vaquero. He wears boots, spurs and a ten-gallon hat and rides a rangy old saddle horse. This is the iconic, romantic image of the cowboy—John Wayne, Roy Rogers and the Lone Ranger. Traditionally, the life of a cowboy was one of hardship. He worked long hours for little pay, the work was tough and dirty, and life was lonely on the wide-open prairies.

The cowboy has also come to be thought of as the imparter of short bursts of wisdom such as, "Always saddle your own horse" or "Never trust a man who agrees with you.

He's probably wrong." As Mark Twain said, "It ain't what you don't know that gets you into trouble. It's what you think you know for sure that just ain't so." Another bit of cowboy wisdom comes from Willie Clement's book *All Hat, No Horse: Cowboy Humor* (2012): "If you're ridin' ahead of the herd, take a look back every now and then to make sure it's still there with ya." A cowboy has a lot of time in the saddle to think of these pearls, and this book tells both about the cowboy and the wisdom he imparts.

Women's Wisdom

Cowboys and cowgirls tend to have a self-deprecating sense of humor. Witness Cindy Shipton's LinkedIn profile, in which she defines herself as a "cook, groundskeeper & bottle washer." Cindy is married to John Gattey of the storied centennial Cross Bar Ranch, near Consort, Alberta, and is too modest to lay claim to her many fine qualities.

 COWBOY WISDOM

"Treat a woman like a racehorse, and she'll never be a nag."

The Cowboy Defined

The *Oxford Dictionary* defines a cowboy as "a person who herds and tends cattle, especially in the western U.S." For some reason, the significance of cowboys in Canada isn't mentioned in dictionaries. Cowboys, however, played a very prominent role in the settlement of western Canada, particularly Alberta, but also British Columbia and Saskatchewan.

Interestingly, in the present-day colloquial sense, a cowboy is someone who is unscrupulous or reckless in his or her business dealings. There are some who might say that the cowboy is an urban myth in the 21st century, but they would be wrong.

Hugh Dempsey says it well in his book *The Golden Age of the Canadian Cowboy* (1965). To quote: "Over the years, the American cowboy has been both romanticized and vilified by movies, television and novels to the point where the image and reality have little in common." As Dempsey goes on to say, the Canadian cowboy was a hardworking man with special skills: "He was deft with a rope, handy with a branding iron and had an intimate knowledge of cattle, horses and his surroundings. As a rule he was tough, hardy and fiercely loyal."

By Any Other Name

There are a number of synonyms for "cowboy." A few of the more popular ones include "cowherd," "herdsman," "cowpuncher" and "wrangler."

 COWBOY WISDOM
"A cowboy is a man with guts and a horse."

The Calgary Stampede

The "Greatest Outdoor Show on Earth," better known as the Calgary Stampede, owes its origins to cowboys and attracts millions of visitors annually. The Calgary Stampede is over 100 years old; in 1912, American promoter Guy Weadick organized the first rodeo and festival in Calgary and called it the Stampede.

COWBOYS PERSONIFIED

Traditional cowboy, circa 1939

The Real McCoy

You can spot a true cowboy a mile away by the way he dresses and behaves. He'll be wearing cowboy boots, blue jeans, a wide belt with a large cowboy buckle, probably a plaid shirt if it's a dress occasion, definitely long-sleeved, with a Stetson cowboy hat on his head. Some prefer felt hats and others straw ones, depending on the season. Usually, he'll have a "farmer's tan" and a weathered look, sometimes with a bit of stubble on his cheeks. Cowboys are often stocky when young and a bit on the lean side as they age. They tend to be quiet and are generally not known to be showboats. A cowboy is almost always very polite and respectful, unless he has good reason to be riled—then watch out. He can be tough as nails and does not suffer fools gladly. A cowboy tends to be conservative and often sees things in black and white. Nowadays, he often drives a pickup truck with an open box. Don't be surprised if there's a box of .22-caliber rifle shells on the dashboard to deal with wayward pests.

 ## Cowboy Wisdom
"Never miss a good chance to shut up."

The Cowboy Character

During an evening out at Edmonton's popular Sorrentino's Downtown restaurant as the 40th annual 2013 Canadian Finals Rodeo was wrapping up, I spoke with general manager Michael Sayde about his cowboy attire. He was all decked out in blue jeans, cowboy shirt, bolo tie, tan leather vest and black Stetson. I commented on his attire and asked him what he thought about cowboys. He was quick to say, "I really admire cowboys. They're hardworking, patient; they're determined and perseverant."

Michael's comments brought back memories of an interview I had with Alberta's Cross Bar Ranch owner John Gattey for an article in *Canadian Cowboy Country* magazine regarding his 10,000-acre (4047-hectare) spread.

This ranch started in 1910 with a saddle horse and a $100 brand, with an eye to the future, and it is now over 100 years old. John recollected his dad, Frank, saying, "You don't quit just because you're tired…if you haven't got the job done, you better go finish it."

DID YOU  KNOW?

The Cowboy Way is a 1994 comedy film directed by Gregg Champion and starring Woody Harrelson and Kiefer Sutherland. The plot follows two championship rodeo stars and lifelong best friends, Pepper Lewis (Harrelson) and Sonny Gilstrap (Sutherland), as they travel from New Mexico to New York in search of their missing friend, Nacho Salazar, who came to the city to pay for his daughter's trip to the U.S. from Cuba. When they discover that he's been murdered, the pair set out to find the killer.

The Real Cowboy Way

John Steber puts it well in his book *Cowboys* (1988) in the "Cowboy Way" chapter: "In this civilized day and age we have rodeos, dude ranches, books, magazines, television specials and movies dedicated to the cowboy. But being a cowboy is not something you see in an arena or on the printed page or the screen. It is something that grows from within. It is a way of life."

DID YOU  KNOW?

"Get the hell out of Dodge" means to leave somewhere immediately. The saying refers to Dodge City, Kansas, a favorite location for western movies and TV series in the early to mid-20th century. The phrase was made famous by the TV show *Gunsmoke*, in which the bad guys were told to "Get the hell out of Dodge" by quiet-spoken Marshal Matt Dillon, played by James Arness. The phrase was popular in the 1960s and '70s.

Hollywood Cowboys

Hollywood personalities such as John Wayne have embodied all that is good about cowboys—characteristically, they're highly regarded for their honesty, for being of sound character and the antithesis of villains. They're also hardworking and tough—what we like to think of as unqualified heroes often known for rescuing unfortunate people. In short, cowboys tend to be men of their word who mean what they say.

Listen and Learn

I've known a lot of ranchers in my home province of Alberta. Typically, they're people of few words, often too busy to get into long-winded discussions. If you listen to them carefully, though (and read between the lines), they usually have an important subliminal message—pay attention because they know what they're talking about. These men work hard in a competitive business and do not suffer fools gladly; they're survivors in a cutthroat society.

Tom Mix at horse show, 1925

Hollywood's *First* Western Movie Star: Thomas E. "Tom" Mix (1880–1940)

Thomas Edwin "Tom" Mix (born Thomas Hezikiah Mix) was a handsome American film actor and the star of many early western movies. He was Hollywood's first western megastar and is notable for having helped define the genre for all the cowboy actors who followed. Between 1909 and 1935, Mix appeared in an astounding 291 films, all but nine of which were silent movies.

DID YOU KNOW?

After working at a variety of odd jobs in the Oklahoma Territory, Mix found employment at the Miller Brothers 101 Ranch, one of the largest ranching businesses in the United States. The ranch covered 101,000 acres (40,870 hectares), hence its name. Mix was a skilled horseman and expert shot, winning national riding and roping contests at Prescott, Arizona, in 1909, and Cañon City, Colorado, in 1910.

Greenhorns, Dudes, Mavericks and Wranglers

Cowboys have spawned an eclectic vocabulary that's become part of everyday conversation in America and Canada. For example, the expression "greenhorn" is used in the same way as "green" to refer to someone as being new. Ranchers coined the term to describe someone who is new to the job and has never roped cattle before, though it can be applied to anyone who is inexperienced. Canadian cowboys called greenhorns "T. Eaton cowboys," a forerunner of the later term "drugstore cowboys."

The word "dude" was often used to describe a lazy, useless youth who affected the dress of a bona fide cowboy to impress others but probably never did any meaningful cowboy work.

A "maverick" is defined as "an unorthodox or independent-minded person" or "one that refuses to abide by the dictates of or resists adherence to a group; a dissenter." It arises from the cowboy use of the word to describe "an unbranded range animal, especially a calf that has become separated from its mother, traditionally considered the property of the first person who brands it."

A "wrangler" is typically defined as "a person in charge of horses or other livestock on a ranch" or "a person engaging in a lengthy and complicated quarrel or dispute," while "a wrangle" is "a dispute or argument, typically one that is long and complicated."

Famous One-liners

Some of the better-known one-liners that are common in today's vocabulary originated from western movie actors like John Wayne and Clint Eastwood. Even phrases uttered by characters in long-ago westerns are still in use. As the Lone Ranger (played by Clayton Moore) departed on his white stallion, Silver, in the finale of each episode of the TV series, he would shout out, "Hi-yo, Silver! Away!" Then as they galloped off, someone would ask, "Who was that masked man, anyway?" Tonto usually referred to the Lone Ranger as "Ke-mo sah-bee," a name that meant either "trusty scout" or "trusted friend." These particular catchphrases, the Lone Ranger's trademark silver bullets and the theme music of the *William Tell Overture* have become part of contemporary popular culture even though *The Lone Ranger* television series ran many years ago, from 1949 to 1957.

Wayne's Words

John Wayne, as the character of Tom Donovan in the movie *The Man Who Shot Liberty Valance*, used the word "pilgrim" when talking to Ransom Stoddard (played by Jimmy Stewart). He called Stoddard "pilgrim," because Stoddard was heading out West to settle in the new territories that had not yet become official states, in much the same way the original Pilgrims came to America. The movie is the flashback story of a tenderfoot who becomes a success by shooting an outlaw who was terrorizing his town. Stewart personified the qualities of a soft-spoken but tough hero in this film.

Another one of John Wayne's famous quotes was "Young fella, if you're looking for trouble, I'll accommodate ya," from the celebrated 1969 western *True Grit*.

DID YOU KNOW?

John Wayne, a likeable and popular Hollywood star, played in a total of 250 movies and was nominated for three Oscars during his acting career. He received the 1969 Academy Award for Best Actor for his performance as U.S. Marshal Rooster Cogburn in *True Grit*.

CATTLE DRIVES

Modern cattle roundup

On the Trail

For clarification, cattle were "trailed," not driven. They were guided in a certain direction as they grazed and were not actually driven unless it was necessary to reach food and water. The real drive was done on the first day on the trail when the cattle were pushed to their limit to get them off their home range and tire them into submission. When the cattle became used to traveling in a herd on the trail, they were said to be "herd broke" or "trail broke." In every cattle herd, there was a dominant steer that took his place at the head of the group and remained the leader until the end of the drive. Some herd steers were valued so much that they were driven back home and used on the next trail drive.

Eastward, Ho!

Cattle drives were a major economic activity in the American West, particularly between 1866 and 1886 after the Civil War (1861–65), when some 20 million cattle were herded from Texas through Indian Territory (now the state of Oklahoma) to railheads in Kansas and Missouri to be shipped to stockyards in Chicago and eastern markets. At the time, the demand for beef outpaced the supply in the northeastern United States because the region had a large population and its cattle herds had been greatly reduced by the ravages of the Civil War. On the other hand, the supply of cattle in Texas was greater than the demand for beef. The long distances covered, the need for periodic rests by riders and animals and the establishment of railheads led to the development of "cow towns" along cattle drive routes across the American West. Because of the subsequent extensive coverage of cattle drives in fiction and film, the cowboy became an iconic image of the United States.

Driving Speed

Although cattle could be driven as far as 24 miles (40 kilometers) a day, they would lose so much weight that they would be hard to sell when they reached the end of the trail. Usually they were taken a shorter distance each day and allowed periods to rest and graze both at midday and at night. On average, a herd could maintain a healthy weight moving about 15 miles (24 kilometers) per day. At such a pace, it could take as long as a couple of months to travel from a home ranch to a railhead. For example, the Chisholm Trail between Kansas and Texas was 994 miles (1600 kilometers) long and would take at least two months to traverse. This trail was in use from 1867 until 1882.

Trail Songs

The famed Chisholm Trail is the subject of at least two country songs. "The Last Cowboy Song" is about a time on the trail before fences led to the end of the great cattle drives.

It was written and recorded by Ed Bruce (1980) and also performed by The Highwaymen.

The song "The Old Chisholm Trail," which dates back to the 1870s, has been covered by a number of western singers, including Gene Autry, Girls of the Golden West, Woody Guthrie, Michael Martin Murphey, Tex Ritter, Roy Rogers and Lead Belly (Huddie Ledbetter), who titled his version "When I Was a Cowboy." "The Old Chisholm Trail" features a catchy chorus: "Coma ti yi youpy, youpy yea, youpy yea, Coma ti yi youpy, youpy yea."

DID YOU KNOW?

Two movies depict an account of the first drive along the Chisholm Trail: *The Texans* (1938), directed by James Hogan and starring Randolph Scott and Joan Bennett; and *Red River* (1948), directed by Howard Hawks and starring John Wayne and Montgomery Clift. Walter Brennan co-starred in both films in his usual cantankerous supporting role.

The Trail Team

Generally, a single herd of cattle on a long drive numbered about 2000 to 3000 head. To herd the cattle, a crew of at least 8 to 12 cowboys was needed, led by a **trail boss**. Each cowboy had three horses so that a fresh mount was always available. The horse herd of fresh mounts was known as the *remuda*, a Spanish word for "remount."

A **wrangler** cared for the crew's horses. Usually the wrangler's job was considered the most menial position in a cattle drive, and he'd also help the cook gather wood and hitch his teams. The wrangler on a cattle drive was often a very young cowboy or one of lower social status, and being a wrangler was an apprenticeship of sorts before moving up the pecking order.

Remuda, circa 1904

Cowboys worked in shifts to watch the cattle 24 hours a day, herding them in the proper direction in the daytime and watching them at night to prevent stampedes and deter theft. A day on the trail started before sunrise. The trail boss led the cattle drive and rode far ahead to survey the lay of the land and search out watering holes and good grazing grounds. Two experienced cowboys called **point men** were positioned behind the trail boss to act as pilots to help guide the herd. Being a point man was an honored position; it was the station of greatest responsibility because these two men determined the exact direction taken by the herd. When they wanted the herd to change direction, the point men would ride abreast of the foremost cattle, then quietly veer in the desired direction; the lead cattle would swerve away from the horseman that was approaching them and toward the one that was receded from them.

Two **swing men** rode alongside the herd, and a couple of **flank men** rode toward the rear. Usually three or four **drag men** traveled behind the herd to corral strays and block cattle from wandering away. The drag men ate dust most of the day, and this job was one of the least desirable on a cattle drive.

Camp cook, circa 1939

The crew also included a **cook**, who drove a chuckwagon, usually pulled by oxen. The cook was a key member of the crew; not only was he in charge of the food, but he was also in charge of medical supplies and typically had a working knowledge of practical medicine. The cook traveled ahead of the cattle drive and had meals prepared when the crew stopped for the night at about 5:00 PM.

DID YOU  KNOW?

According to Hugh Dempsey's book *The Golden Age of the Canadian Cowboy* (1995), "When working on the range, no one was supposed to ride ahead of the man leading the circle. Everyone followed the boss until told or motioned with a jerk of the thumb what to do. On riding into camp, everyone was careful to approach downwind from the fire and cooking pots. The space between the mess wagon and the fire was sacred ground—the cook's private domain."

RANCHING IN BRITISH COLUMBIA

Canada's First Cattle Industry

The British Columbia cattle industry was actually the first to be developed in Canada. The initial movement of cattle to the province probably occurred in 1846, when Dr. John McLoughlin, chief factor of the Hudson's Bay Company, moved cattle and horses from Fort Vancouver at the mouth of the Columbia River by boat to Vancouver Island and then to what was then Fort Kamloops and Fort Alexandria. Small herds of beef and dairy cattle were kept at Fort Kamloops, Fort Alexandria, Fort Victoria and Fort Langley.

The town of Barkerville had a population of 10,000 at the height of the Cariboo Gold Rush (circa 1865). Cattle were driven north to feed the hungry prospectors.

Cattle Crossing

The discovery of gold on the Fraser River and the expiration of the Hudson's Bay Company trading license in 1858 signaled the beginnings of settlement in British Columbia. A couple of months after the first American miners crossed the Canada-U.S. border, General Joel Palmer of California crossed the border at Osoyoos from Fort Okanogan in the Washington Territory and traveled through the Okanagan Valley and on to the Thompson Valley with a cattle drive and wagons pulled by oxen. The following year, he took another cattle drive as far as Fort Alexandria on the Fraser River. Over the next decade, about 22,000 head of cattle were brought from the Oregon Territory, mostly to the Barkerville mines.

The First Ranches

Settlement first occurred in linear form in the early 1860s along the Brigade and other cattle drive trails, as well as along the Cariboo Road. Ranching got its start in BC at about the same time. The Alkali Lake Ranch was established in 1861, followed by the 150 Mile Ranch, also in 1861, then the 100 Mile Ranch in 1863 and the Gang Ranch in 1863–80. The Okanagan Mission was founded near Kelowna in 1859. Many of the ranches were established by well-educated, middle-class British immigrants who brought their own traditions and culture with them, including riding with the hounds and playing polo.

The British Columbia Cattlemen's Association

The British Columbia Cattlemen's Association has been representing BC ranchers since 1929. The province's cattle industry is made up primarily of cow-calf operations, and there are about 4086 cattle ranches operating in BC, which make up five percent of Canada's national cowherd.

RANCHING ON THE PRAIRIES

The Americans Come North

According to Hugh Dempsey's book *The Golden Age of the Canadian Cowboy* (1995), the golden age of the cowboy on the Canadian prairies extends from 1880 to "the disastrous winter" of 1906–07. In 1886, the Americans drove about 30,000 head of cattle across the border into Canada, but a terrible winter that year devastated the herds and dampened the Americans' enthusiasm to expand their range northward. Although cowboys thrived after this time, the influx of settlers onto the Canadian prairies and the breakup of the large ranches into smaller holdings changed his role forever.

Cypress Hills, Alberta

Wide-open Spaces

Canada's potential prime ranching area was along the Alberta foothills and east of the Cypress Hills and Maple Creek regions in Saskatchewan. These key areas were out of the reach of ranching interests until treaties were made with

Canadian First Nations tribes (starting with the signing of Treaty 7 in southern Alberta in 1877) and the plains bison no longer dominated the native ranges.

DID YOU KNOW?

Treaty 7 is one of 11 numbered treaties signed between Canada's First Nations and the Crown between 1871 and 1921.

The Start of the Big Spreads

Most of the formative ranchers came from eastern Canada and Britain; however, there were also American ranches, such as the Circle and the Spencers from Montana, the McIntyre's from Utah and the Matador from California. These ranches operated on a scale that was comparable to the founding ranches in Alberta such as the Cochrane, the Walrond and the Oxley, which were of British and eastern Canadian origin.

DID YOU KNOW?

Canadian ranches started with Texas longhorns and rangy mixes of Shorthorns and Durhams, but the owners of large ranches quickly upgraded their stock using purebred bulls.

Cowboy Wisdom

"Behind every successful rancher is a wife who works in town."

Early Alberta Ranchers

Some of Alberta's most successful early settlers were ranchers who discovered that the southwestern foothills area of the province was ideal livestock country, and it remains a center of Alberta's contemporary beef cattle industry. In this area, the sheltered, well-watered valleys and the Chinook winds that bare the hills of winter snow combine to make it one of North America's preferred cattle-raising areas. However, there was an old cowboy saying, "Don't go north of the Bow River," a caution that conditions were not as favorable farther north during Alberta's long winters.

British Ranches and American Cowboys

Many of Alberta's ranching pioneers were from the United Kingdom, but the cowboys—such as the infamous John Ware who brought the first cattle to Alberta—were primarily from the United States. These cowboys had a reputation for working hard and playing hard.

DID YOU KNOW?

When a stranger rode into a cow camp, he was invited to "pull his saddle off and come an' eat," but, as a matter of range etiquette, he was never asked his name or where he came from.

The NWMP Keeps the Peace

After 1874, the North-West Mounted Police provided the key essentials of an incipient range cattle industry: a small local market and security for open grazing. The NWMP was soon joined by Joseph MacFarland, an Irish American frontiersman, and George Emerson, a former Hudson's Bay man, who drove small herds in from Montana. At the same time, in the Bow River valley west of Fort Calgary, George and John McDougall established a cattle herd near their mission at Morleyville (present-day Morley).

DID YOU  KNOW?

Brothels were common in southern Alberta towns near the turn of the last century. Lethbridge was one of the most wide-open towns, with a half-dozen brightly painted brothels operating at a place called "The Point," the area on the west end of Fourth Avenue South, behind the site of the present-day Lethbridge Lodge Hotel. The most notorious bordello was run by a woman named Carrie McLean, commonly called "Cowboy Jack," who originally hailed from Montana. Prostitution was also very common in Calgary at that time.

From Cop to Cattleman

Numerous former mounted policemen joined the ranching fraternity when their terms of enlistment expired, and they formed a distinctive core about which the industry developed, helping to define its emerging social character.

Gentlemen Ranchers

The British Canadian orientation of the ranching frontier was reinforced by the arrival of Englishmen attracted by the great publicity accorded in Britain to North American cattle ranching. They typically described themselves as "gentlemen" and came generally from the landed gentry, with sufficient capital to establish their own ranches.

Rails to Ranches

Access to distant markets was assured when the Canadian Pacific Railway finally reached the Prairies in the early 1880s and interest in ranching grew dramatically. Led by Montréal capitalist and stockbreeder Senator Matthew Cochrane, Canadian businessmen vied to obtain the grazing leases provided through the Dominion Lands Policy of 1876. The lure of being able to ship western Canadian beef to the rapidly expanding British market and cashing in on the cattle bonanza led Cochrane and others to organize the great cattle companies that soon dominated the Canadian range: the Cochrane, Bar U, Oxley and Walrond ranches in Alberta; the 76, Hitchcock and Matador ranches in Saskatchewan; and the Douglas Lake, Gang and Empire Valley ranches in BC.

Alberta's Western Stock Growers Association

Alberta's Western Stock Growers Association, founded in 1896, remains a key advocate for ranchers in the province, along with the Alberta Beef Producers, which was established in 1874. The main priority of the Western Stock Growers Association is to protect livestock producers by lobbying the government through written submissions, briefs and presentations on behalf of the cattle industry. Membership is voluntary, which the association claims ensures that their agenda is member-focused. The organization hosts a reward fund, which provides rewards of up to $50,000 for information leading to the arrest and conviction of any person or persons stealing livestock from a member.

From the U.S. to Saskatchewan

According to the *Atlas of Saskatchewan* (1969), in the late 1800s, Americans primarily from Texas, Montana and Arizona herded cattle to the Cypress Hills and the Big Muddy Badlands area. For example, the Manitoba Land Investments Corporation began as an American land company and played a role in early ranching in Saskatchewan.

American ranching companies were established in southern Saskatchewan between 1881 and 1906, after the decline of the buffalo and after Canadian leasehold legislation was passed to promote ranching. Some of the companies included Olivier's

Ranch NW 15-41-25 on the Fort Qu'Appelle Touchwood Trail; McKenzies' Ranch near Basin Lake; Venne Ranch in Menaginous Hills; the Turkey Track, managed by A.J. Tony Day, one of several ranches near Hallonquist; the 76 Ranch near Swift Current (there were actually 10 ranches of the 76 brand between Swift Current, Saskatchewan, and Calgary, Alberta, and they were mainly located between Maple Creek, Saskatchewan, and the U.S.-Canada border); the Matador Ranch, which was based in Texas and leased land in Saskatchewan; the Gull Lake Ranching Company, managed by James G. Millar; the Circle Diamond spread in the flat of Frenchman Creek; and the Wayne Ranch, run by Campbell McCutcheon.

American ranches prospered around Swift Current and Maple Creek, Saskatchewan, and Medicine Hat, Alberta, supplying horses for the Boer War in 1900 and for the 1896 Klondike Gold Rush. Many Montana ranchers in the Eastend area departed after the devastating winter of 1906–07.

Economic Importance

Ranching remains extremely important to the provincial economy, especially in southwestern Saskatchewan, where about 40 percent of the land is native rangeland.

Saskatchewan Stock Growers Association

The Saskatchewan Stock Growers Association is a non-profit organization established in 1913 to represent the cattle industry on the legislative front. The association safeguards the interests of producers by working to defeat or amend proposals that would affect the industry in Saskatchewan.

DID YOU KNOW?

To commemorate their 100th anniversary in 2013, the Saskatchewan Stock Growers Association marketed 100th-anniversary belt buckles and a limited edition print entitled *Riding for the Brand* by Bernie Brown, a self-taught pencil artist born and raised in Saskatchewan.

RANCHING IN THE UNITED STATES

Ranch near Spur, Texas, circa 1939

From Mexico Northward

Cattle ranching in North America got its start in Mexico and later became a dominant industry in Texas mainly because of suitable range conditions. Mild winter weather meant that cattle could graze on unfenced land or open ranges during fall and winter. During the Civil War, cattle in the state were left to run wild. Because the natural conditions were so favorable, the herd grew quickly, and by 1865, there were over six million cattle in Texas.

An Emerging Industry

To satisfy a growing market, particularly in the eastern United States, in 1867, several thousand cattle were driven northward to places such as Dodge City, Wichita, Newton, Abilene and Ellsworth, where they were loaded on trains bound for St. Louis, Kansas City and Chicago, after which they were shipped to farther eastern markets and even to Great Britain to feed a growing population. At the time, cattle that sold for $3 or $6 a head in Texas could be sold for $38 a head in Kansas or $80 in New York. Starting in the spring, when the grass turned green, cattle were later trailed north of Texas along the Chisholm Trail, the Western Trail and other cattle trails to such distant places as Montana, the Dakota Territories and Canada. Along the way, they grazed on the open range. During one particularly large cattle drive in 1866, cowboys moved about 260,000 head north along the Sedalia Trail, later known as the Shawnee Trail, from south Texas through Indian Territory to Sedalia, Missouri.

Forging Trails

The Chisholm Trail was originally blazed by Jesse Chisholm in the mid-1860s, and in 1867, Texas cowboys trailed 35,000 longhorns from southern Texas to Abilene, Kansas. The Western Trail was forged in 1874 and went from southern Texas to Dodge City in southwestern Kansas. By 1879, the Western Trail was the main route used for moving Texas cattle to market. It's been estimated that over six million cattle were moved out of Texas on these trails during the heyday of the cattle drives.

Goodnight-Loving and Other Trails

Not all cattle trails ended at stockyards in Kansas and Missouri for eastern markets. The Goodnight-Loving Trail, which went from Texas through New Mexico into Colorado, was used to supply cattle to cavalry posts, Native American reservations and Colorado gold mines. There were other cattle drive routes elsewhere in the West, such as over the Oregon Trail from Missouri to Oregon Country and to Montana through Miles City.

DID YOU  KNOW?

In the decade from 2002 to 2012, the number of cattle in Texas declined from about 14 million to 12 million.

From East to West

As settlers moved westward in the United States from the east coast, they brought cattle breeds from that area and Europe along with them. They later adapted range management practices to the drier lands of the West by borrowing key elements of the Spanish *vaquero* culture. Although there are many forms of range management in the West, most rely on a system of rest and rotational grazing to allow native plants to recover and to seed out before grazing resumes.

DID YOU  KNOW?

There were cattle on the Eastern Seaboard long before the West was settled. Deep Hollow Ranch, 111 miles (180 kilometers) east of New York City in Montauk, New York, claims to be the first ranch in the United States, in continuous operation since 1658, though this is debatable.

Home on the Open Range

The vast, open prairie and desert lands of what today is Mexico and the western United States were well-suited to open-range cattle grazing. Free-ranging plains bison had roamed throughout the Canadian Prairies and the American Great Plains for centuries. Likewise, cattle and sheep, descended from animals brought over from Europe, were simply turned loose in the spring after their young were born and allowed to roam with little supervision and no fences, then rounded up in the fall. The mature animals were driven to market and the breeding stock was brought close to the ranch headquarters for greater protection in the winter. Cattle branding allowed the cattle owned by different ranchers to be identified and sorted. Beginning with the settlement of Texas in the 1840s and expansion both north and west from that time, through the Civil War and into the 1880s, ranching dominated western economic activity.

The fencing of property ended the days of open-range grazing.

The End of Open-range Grazing

Contrary to popular belief, the end of the open range was not brought about by a reduction in land because of crop farming, but by overgrazing. Cattle that were stocked on the open range created a "tragedy of the commons" as each rancher sought increased economic benefit by grazing too many animals on public lands that nobody owned. The winter of 1886–87 was one of the most severe on record, and live-stock that were already stressed by reduced grazing died by the thousands. Many large cattle operations went bankrupt, and others suffered severe financial losses. Consequently, after this time, ranchers began to fence off their land and negotiated individual grazing leases with the U.S. government so that they could keep better control of the pasture-land available to their own animals. Prior to this, farmers had already opted to fence off their property with barbed wire to protect their crops from wandering cattle. In particu-lar, farmers in eastern Kansas and Missouri had to resort to fencing because cattle drives sometimes trampled their crops.

DID YOU KNOW?

With the invention of barbed wire in 1874 and an influx of settlers who staked out waterholes and cut up the open range, the heyday of big cattle outfits and their cowboys became history.

Early Ranching in Arizona

The Arizona Heritage Traveler website sheds some light on the history of pioneer ranching in the West. Ranching began in Arizona with the arrival of the Spanish conquistadors, who introduced cattle to southern Arizona and established vast land grant haciendas such as the Arivaca, Reventon, Sopori and Canoa along the Santa Cruz River and the San Bernardino River in the southeastern corner of the state. The first American to establish an Arizona cattle ranch was William Kirkland, who started operations in 1857 in Canoa, about 20 miles (32 kilometers) north of Tubac. In 1862, William S. Oury introduced purebred cattle at his Tanque Verde ranch east of Tucson. Today the Tanque Verde is a well-known guest ranch. When ex-military men and miners poured into Arizona after the Civil War, the demand for meat escalated, and ranching soon spread from the valleys of the Santa Cruz and the San Pedro rivers in the south to land along the Little Colorado River in the north. In addition, the cattle industry was bolstered by government contracts to feed the Native Americans that they had moved to reservations in Arizona and New Mexico.

ALBERTA RANCHES

Cross Bar Ranch family: John Gattey with sons Brandon and Justin

Ranch Roundup

There are many notable ranches in Alberta, particularly "century ranches"—ranches that have been continuously owned and operated by a single family for a minimum of 100 years—such as Bennett Ranches Ltd., E&G Maser Farming and Ranching Ltd., the Cross Bar Ranch, McIntyre Ranch and Mesabi Ranches Inc., and also those of historical importance like the A7, Cochrane and Bar U ranches. Other key ranches still operating are the Stampede Ranch, the OH Ranch, the Waldron Ranch and the Ya Ha Tinda ranch.

DID YOU  KNOW?

The owners of century ranches can apply to be recognized by the Alberta government. The provincial Department of

Agriculture and Rural Development lists recipients of the Alberta Century Farm and Ranch Award on their website at www.agric.gov.ab.ca/app68/centuryfarm. Please note that it is up to the farm and ranch families to apply for this award themselves, otherwise they won't be listed on the website.

Senator Matthew Cochrane

Cochrane Ranche

The settlement of western Canada lacked the raw frontier roughness that was experienced in the American West. Rather, the policies of Conservative Party leader and first

Canadian prime minister Sir John A. Macdonald, who was elected in 1867, focused on controlled settlement of the region. Government policy catered to the creation of a Canadian ranching elite with leases up to 100,000 acres (40,468 hectares) in size under an amendment to the Dominion Lands Act of 1867. The first grazing lease was issued to the pioneer Cochrane Ranche in 1881, which was incorporated by eastern capitalists under Senator Matthew Cochrane of Quebec. The Cochrane Ranche paid $500,000 for a huge lease that straddled the proposed route of the Canadian Pacific Railway along the Bow River and that also encompassed ideal grazing land west of Calgary. By 1882, there were 12,000 cattle on the spread. Subsequent events resulted in the ranch holdings being split up and relocated farther south.

Stampede Ranch

The Calgary Stampede purchased its own ranch in 1961. Located east of Hanna in eastern Alberta, the property covers a total of 22,000 acres (8903 hectares) and has 500 horses and 80 bulls. Elite animals of the rodeo world share the pastureland with whitetail and mule deer, pronghorn antelope and many species of birds and small mammals. Bullpound Creek meanders through 6 miles (10 kilometers) of the ranchland, and there are six types of native and cultivated grass for grazing.

OH Ranch

The 8000-acre (3237-hectare) OH Ranch is a 130-year-old working cattle ranch on the Highwood River west of Longview. It was donated to the Calgary Stampede Foundation in 2012, at which time the Calgary Stampede became the new steward of the ranch. The Calgary Stampede is committed to preserving this working ranch and protecting its natural environment and heritage value.

Waldron Ranch

The 30,535-acre (12,357-hectare) Waldron Ranch is located on the eastern slopes of the Rocky Mountains in southwestern Alberta along the Oldman River. The ranch is bisected by Highway 22, the Cowboy Trail. In 2013, a co-operative of 72 Alberta ranchers entered into an agreement with the Nature Conservancy of Canada to protect the land against development, subdivision, cultivation or drainage. The $37.5 million purchase of a conservation easement was officially announced on September 11, 2013, after two years of negotiation with the grazing co-op. It is the largest Canadian landscape ever to be conserved by an easement. The property will remain a working ranch.

Ya Ha Tinda Ranch

The 9748-acre (3944-hectare) Ya Ha Tinda Ranch is located along the north bank of the Red Deer River adjacent to Banff National Park. The ranch is private property and has been owned and managed by Parks Canada as pasture for their horses since 1917. It is the only federally operated working horse ranch in Canada. Horses are wintered and trained on the Ya Ha Tinda Ranch to be used as working horses for patrolling and protecting Canada's western national parks.

BRITISH COLUMBIA RANCHES

Alkali Lake Ranch

Billed as the oldest ranch in BC, the Alkali Lake Ranch is located 31 miles (50 kilometers) south of Williams Lake. It's believed to be the first cattle ranch established in western Canada and is one of the largest in BC. It covers 37,000 deeded acres (14,973 hectares) and the ranch's range permit encompasses about 125,000 acres (50,585 hectares). Founded in 1861 by German-born Herman Otto Bowe, the ranch remained in his family until 1910; that year, it was sold to an Englishman, Charles Wynn Johnson, who added to the holdings over the next 30 years. Mario Reidemann, an Austrian business magnate, purchased the ranch in 1939, and his son Martin took over the operation in 1963. In 1977, the Mervyn family from Kelowna became the new owners. The ranch is presently, and always has been, privately operated.

Douglas Lake Ranch

Founded in 1886, the Douglas Lake Ranch is Canada's largest working ranch. Approximately 515,000 acres (208,413 hectares) in size, it has about 18,000 head of cattle and employs approximately 60 people. The Douglas Lake Ranch traces its name back to 1872, when John Douglas Sr. homesteaded his first 320 acres (129 hectares) along the shore of Douglas Lake. In 1884, he sold the property to Charles Beak, who, along with Joseph Greaves, Charles Thomson and William Ward founded the Douglas Lake Cattle Company on June 30, 1886. Douglas Lake Ranch is located 32 miles (52 kilometers) east of Merritt and 58 miles (93 kilometers) south of Kamloops.

DID YOU KNOW?

The Douglas Lake Ranch boasts some of the best fly-fishing in British Columbia. The ranch even operates a general store and post office!

Gang Ranch

The famous and historic Gang Ranch is located in the Chilcotin region of British Columbia, 28 miles (45 kilometers) north of Clinton on the west bank of the Fraser River. The ranch was founded in 1863 by two American brothers, Thaddeus and Jerome Harperin. For many years the largest ranch in North America, the Gang Ranch is now the second largest in Canada, after the Douglas Lake Ranch. It consisted of one million acres (404,685 hectares) in 1974 and pastured 4000 cattle in the 1990s.

It's not certain where the name Gang Ranch originated. The ranch may have been named for the large double-furrow plow called a "gang plow," which was pulled by several teams of workhorses, or for the number of workers it took to run a place of this size.

DID YOU KNOW?

There are unconfirmed reports that Microsoft founder, Bill Gates, once looked into buying the Gang Ranch.

SASKATCHEWAN RANCHES

Gilchrist Brothers Ranch

According to the *Encyclopedia of Saskatchewan*, the Gilchrist Brothers Ranch was the largest ranch in Canada in the 1940s. Saskatchewan rancher Joe Gilchrist told the author that the Gilchrist Brothers Ranch holdings comprised ranch property in both Alberta (including the Q Ranch and others) and Saskatchewan in 1941.

Matador Ranch

At the turn of the last century, what was then the Q Ranch, near Kyle, Saskatchewan, had extensive operations along the South Saskatchewan River. (There's also a Q Ranch in Alberta, south of the Cypress Hills.) In 1905, 50,000 acres (20,234 hectares) of the ranch's holdings were leased to the Matador Cattle Company, an American firm. The Matador Cattle Company originated in 1885 in Dundee, Scotland, but at the time of leasing, their head office was located in Trinidad, Colorado. The Matador Cattle Company grass-fattened steers and heifers until 1922, when the provincial government, under pressure from farmers and ranchers, rendered their holdings into a community pasture.

DID YOU KNOW?

In processing the records of what was known as the Matador Project, Tim Hutchinson, of the University of Saskatchewan archives, came upon the last will and testament of one James

Barnet Henson, who worked on the Matador Ranch.
The document features a humorous codicil:

> "This is a Codicil to my Last Will and Testament
> bearing date the 28th day of September 1919, and
> which I direct to be a part thereof. I give, devise &
> bequeath to George Winser my Navajo saddle-blanket;
> to William Vincent Smith my rope; to Pete LaPlante
> my rifle, in recognition of the fact that they are
> respectively the best rider, the best foot-roper and the
> best shot in the Hills. Finally I leave to each & every
> Mossback [a mossback is defined a person living in
> the backwoods] my perpetual curse, as some reward
> to them for their labors in destroying the Open Range,
> by means of that most pernicious of all implements,
> the plow. As witness my hand this the 9th day of
> May 1922."

Turkey Track Ranch

The Turkey Track Ranch, located in southwestern
Saskatchewan, takes its name from a Texas brand registered
in 1840. The ranch is currently run by Terry and Doug
Ostrander and has been owned by the family since 1917.
Terry is a director on the Saskatchewan Stock Growers
Association board of directors. In 1996, then-owners Jim
and Louise Ostrander and their family received an environ-
mental stewardship award from the Saskatchewan Stock
Growers Association for their work in preserving native
grasslands within the ranch.

76 Ranch

The 76 Ranch took its name from a cattle brand used by the
Powder River Ranch in Wyoming. In 1889, a young British
nobleman, Sir John Lister-Kaye, bought the Powder River
Ranch's entire herd of 5700 cattle for his land development

along the Canadian Pacific Railway line. He kept the brand and took the name "76" for the ranch, which is located in southwestern Saskatchewan. The cattle were trailed into southern Alberta and shipped to Lister-Kaye's various holdings. In 1890, the Crane Lake farm, one of 10 such farms that made up the 76 Ranch, was turned into the cattle operation's headquarters. Each of the 10 farms is said to have had a two-story house, bunkhouse, stables, machine shed, granary and windmill, blacksmith shop, harness room, cattle shed, sheep shed and piggery.

The 76 Ranch apparently had many disasters and carried on for 20 years before folding. It survived the severe winter of 1906–07, but lost two-thirds of its cattle. The British owners sold the 76 Ranch to Gordon, Ironsides and Fares, a ranching, cattle exporting and meatpacking company, in 1909. In 1921, the 76 Ranch was permanently broken up, and the brand passed through a number of owners before returning to the local area in 1945. The 76 Ranch still continues today near Piapot, Saskatchewan.

DID YOU  KNOW?

There's a historical marker at a roadside rest area on Highway 1 in Saskatchewan commemorating the 76 Ranch.

AMERICAN RANCHES

Sierra Bonita Ranch, Arizona

The Sierra Bonita Ranch was the first permanent American cattle ranch in Arizona, located near present-day Willcox in Cochise County. The ranch was first established by Colonel Henry C. Hooker in 1872, on the site of a former Spanish hacienda that was destroyed by the Apaches in the early 19th century. At one time it was the largest ranch in Arizona, totaling 512,000 acres (207,200 hectares).

DID YOU KNOW?

Colonel Hooker became the largest military beef supplier in the Arizona Territory. Over time, he built his holdings until his ranch was home to 20,000 head. He was still the cattle king of Arizona when he died in 1907.

Aztec Land and Cattle Company Ranch, Arizona

The Aztec Land and Cattle Company operated in northern Arizona Territory between 1884 and 1902. In its heyday, the Aztec Company was the third largest cattle company in the United States, with a range spanning over 2 million acres (809,371 hectares) from the border of New Mexico west to an area south of Flagstaff. The company ran some 60,000 head on rangeland that was 40 by 90 miles (64 by 145 kilometers) in area. The ranch bordered the Atlantic and Pacific Railroad line near Holbrook.

DID YOU KNOW?

Many of the cowboys from the Aztec Land and Cattle Company had a reputation for being lawless, particularly in Holbrook, a small town of about 300 people when the company was formed in 1884. In 1886, there were 26 shooting deaths in Holbrook.

Clanton Ranch, Arizona

The Clanton Ranch now bills itself as a luxury fly-fishing lodge. This famous ranch was founded in southern Arizona in 1873 by Newman Haynes "Old Man" Clanton. The horse and cattle ranch was originally located along the San Pedro River south of Tombstone. It became home to some famous cowboys, including Billy the Kid, who worked for the Clantons in about 1873, before he headed for New Mexico.

DID YOU KNOW?

The Parker Ranch is a working cattle ranch on the island of Hawaii and is currently run by a charitable trust. The ranch was founded in 1847 and is one of the oldest ranches in the United States, pre-dating many mainland ranches in Texas and other southwestern states by more than 30 years. By virtue of being 250,000 acres (101,171 hectares) in size, the Parker Ranch is also among the largest cattle ranches in America.

Circle C Ranch, Montana

Walt Coburn wrote a book called *Pioneer Cattleman in Montana: The Story of the Circle C Ranch* (1968) about his father's life and times on this ranch. In 1886, Robert Coburn bought 30,000 acres (12,140 hectares) of land from prospector and cattleman Granville Stuart that lay along Flatwillow Creek in the shadow of the Little Rockies of Montana. He called it a "cattleman's paradise," but a terrible blizzard the following winter erased half of his stock. However, despite long odds, Coburn proved that the Circle C was, indeed, the paradise he envisioned, and he emerged as one of the most progressive men of Montana for his time.

N Bar Ranch, Montana

The N Bar Ranch spans more than 60,000 contiguous acres (24,281 hectares) in the foothills of central Montana's Snowy Mountains, about 90 miles (145 kilometers) north of Billings. The ranch was originally established in 1885 by Thomas Cruse, who had purchased the Montana Sheep Company that same year. The original purchase included 2842 acres (1554 hectares) on Flatwillow Creek at the site of the present-day N Bar Ranch. Following the brutal winter of 1886–87, two brothers, E.S. "Zeke" and Henry H.J. Newman, sold their remaining cattle along with the N Bar brand to Cruse.

Snake River Ranch, Wyoming

The Snake River Ranch is located near Wilson and is the largest deeded ranch in the Jackson Hole area. The ranch combined two homesteads and was first owned by advertising executive Stanley B. Resor and his wife, Helen Lansdowne Resor. The Resors used the property as a vacation home, but the ranch was also a full-time, self-sustaining operation. The Snake River Ranch was listed on the National Register of Historic Places in 2004. It is one of the last working ranches near Jackson Hole and features group ranch tours.

King Ranch, Texas

The King Ranch, located in South Texas between Corpus Christi and Brownsville, is one of the largest ranches in the world. The ranch comprises 825,000 acres (333,865 hectares) and was founded in 1853 by Captain Richard King and Gideon K. Lewis. It includes portions of six Texas counties. The ranch also encompasses large tracts of pristine wildlife habitat, which are used for paid hunting.

DID YOU  KNOW?

The founder of the King Ranch, Richard King (1824–85), was a riverboat captain and entrepreneur. During the Mexican-American War (1846–48), King and a partner ferried army supplies along the Rio Grande and began a steamboat company after the war. He invested his profits in land, purchasing two ranches in 1853 and 1854 that became the nucleus of the King Ranch.

AWESOME

The world's largest ranch, 6 million acres (2.4 million hectares) in area, is Anna Creek Station, located in the Australian state of South Australia. A working cattle station, it is roughly eight times the size of the biggest ranch in the U.S., the King Ranch in Texas.

W. T. Waggoner Ranch, Texas

The largest contiguous ranch in the United States is reportedly the W.T. Waggoner Ranch near Vernon, Texas, and was established in 1849 by Dan Waggoner. The ranch is located 13 miles (21 kilometers) south of Vernon and encompasses approximately 535,000 acres (216,506 hectares).

CATTLEMEN, RANCHERS AND COWBOYS

Literally tomes have been written about famous cowboys, although there is less text regarding famous cowgirls. There have been dozens of cowboys who are considered famous for a number of reasons. Some are known for their notoriety as gunslingers, outlaws and the like or, sadly, for other rather unsavory characteristics, which may explain the checkered modern-era definition of what a cowboy is.

Another, more important category would be cowboys who were leading builders in bygone days. The ones covered in this chapter tend to fall into the categories of either cattlemen, ranchers and cowboys or Wild West show and rodeo performers. Some lawmen of the Old West such as "Bat" Masterson, Wyatt Earp and Pat Garrett (who killed Billy the Kid) might be considered famous cowboys, but they will not be covered here because they fall outside the "cowboy genre."

Gabriel Dumont (1837–1906)

Gabriel Dumont was a charismatic leader of the Métis people in western Canada, notably Saskatchewan. The Métis are one of the recognized Aboriginal groups in Canada and trace their ancestry to mixed First Nations and European heritage. An accomplished shot with both gun and bow by the age of 12, Dumont was also considered a master horseman. He was a key figure of western Canada's Métis community during his lifetime and a close associate of the famous Métis leader Louis Riel. Dumont commanded the Métis rebellion

Gabriel Dumont holding his gun, which he called "le Petit," circa 1880

forces during the North West Rebellion in 1885. He joined Buffalo Bill's Wild West Show in 1886, where he received top billing as a crack shot.

DID YOU  KNOW?

Dumont and his older brother, Isidore, became buffalo hunters. Over time, Dumont learned six languages and established a reputation as a guide, hunter and interpreter. He was also famed for his drinking and gambling. Dumont participated in skirmishes with First Nations/Native American groups, including the Blackfoot and Sioux.

John Ware and family, 1897

John Ware (1845?–1905)

John Ware was an African American cattleman and cowboy, as well as an accomplished horseman and horse trainer. Born a slave in Texas in about 1845, he is best known for bringing the first cattle to southern Alberta in 1883, thereby helping to establish Alberta's ranching industry. Ware was also an accomplished steer-roper and performed at Calgary's first rodeo in 1893. At the time, he was rated as the best bucking horse rider in Canada.

Ware was a big man and reportedly prodigiously strong. His great stature and dedication to hard work made him a natural leader. Ware became a cowboy after the Civil War and came to Canada with the Bar U trail drive in 1882. In the spring of 1883, Ware was contracted by the Bar U Ranch to drive cattle from Lost River, Idaho, to High River, Alberta, and he worked on the ranch until 1884.

Despite being a master horseman, John Ware was killed when his horse tripped in a badger hole, crushing him and breaking his neck when it fell on him. His log ranch house from Duchess, Alberta, is now located in Dinosaur Provincial Park.

AWESOME

In 2012, Canada Post issued a commemorative stamp featuring John Ware to celebrate Black History Month.

DID YOU  KNOW?

Author Hugh Dempsey rates Ware as Canada's most famous black cowboy. One-third of the Old West cowboys were black or Hispanic.

Guy Weadick (1885–1953)

Guy Weadick was a popular American rodeo performer and promoter who worked the vaudeville circuit across North America and Europe, performing rope tricks in a 15-minute western act. Nowadays, he is best known as the founder of the Calgary Stampede in Calgary, Alberta.

In 1912, Guy Weadick organized Calgary's first rodeo and festival, then known as the Stampede. It was held in September, when the ranchers and farmers had finished harvesting and had some free time. Weadick returned to the city in 1919 to organize the Victory Stampede to honor the soldiers returning from World War I. The rodeo became an annual event in 1923, when it merged with the Calgary Industrial Exhibition and became known as the Calgary Exhibition and Stampede. Later, the word "exhibition" was dropped.

Weadick gained financing from a group known as the Big Four in Alberta circles: George Lane, owner of the Bar U Ranch; Patrick Burns and A.E. Cross, both wealthy ranchers; and Archie McLean, the provincial secretary. Billed as "The Greatest Outdoor Show on Earth," the Stampede has grown into a 10-day event held over the Canada Day weekend in July and welcomes over one million visitors annually.

DID YOU KNOW?

The Calgary Stampede's roots actually go back to 1886, when the Calgary and District Agricultural Society held its first fair.

Alfred Ernest (A.E.) Cross (1861–1932)

Politician, rancher and brewer A.E. Cross is probably best known for being one of the Big Four who founded the Calgary Stampede in 1912. Cross moved to Alberta in 1884 to work at a ranch owned by Matthew Henry Cochrane near what is now Cochrane, Alberta. By 1886, Cross owned his own ranch, the A7 Ranche, located near Nanton, Alberta. He established the Calgary Brewing and Malting Company

A.E. Cross, one of the Big Four and a co-founder of the Calgary Stampede

in 1891, the first brewery in what was then the Northwest Territories. That same year, he became a founding member of Calgary's oldest and most exclusive club, the Ranchmen's Club. In the summer of 1912, Cross, along with Patrick Burns, George Lane and Archie McLean (the "Big Four"), put up a total of $100,000 to finance the first Calgary Stampede.

DID YOU  KNOW?

The Big Four Building, named in honor of the Calgary Stampede's benefactors, opened in 1959. It served as the city's largest exhibition hall in the summer and was converted into a 24-sheet curling facility each winter.

Today, this 118,000-square-foot venue features three exhibition halls, meeting rooms and a restaurant.

Patrick Burns (1856–1937)

Patrick Burns was a celebrated rancher, meat packer, businessman, senator and philanthropist. While perhaps best known as a meatpacking magnate, Burns is also credited as being a founding member of the Calgary Stampede. He was one of the first ranchers to stock purebred Hereford cattle, and he pioneered methods for winter feeding cattle. In 1931, he was appointed to the Canadian Senate as a representative for Alberta.

Awesome

On October 16, 2008, the *Calgary Herald* honored Patrick Burns as "Alberta's Greatest Citizen." The accompanying article in the *Herald* stated that "His story is the story of Alberta. His struggles, his dreams, his success and philanthropy define the very core of our western character."

Olaf Olafson (1867–1957)

Born in Iceland in 1867, Olaf Olafson immigrated to western Canada in 1887. After 11 years of railroading with the Canadian Pacific Railway, he took up a homestead at Old Wives, a farm and ranch community near Johnston Lake in the rolling hill country southwest of Moose Jaw, Saskatchewan. According to the Saskatchewan Agricultural Hall of Fame, Olafson was described by a close friend as "a natural-born cattleman." The stock for his ranching enterprise was carefully chosen, and his animals consistently won high awards in the cattle shows of his time. He was a prime mover in the formation of the Saskatchewan Stock Growers Association (SSGA), established in 1913, and became president in 1915.

For most of his long association with the SSGA, Olafson held the positions of president, vice president and honorary president. He also spearheaded a movement to establish much-needed stock-handling facilities at Moose Jaw. With the help of a group of cattlemen from the area, he saw his dream come true when the Southern Saskatchewan Co-operative Stockyards opened in 1918. It soon became the largest operation of its kind in the province. Olafson made the first delivery of cattle to the yards and served as vice president of the institution until 1934. In that year, he was elected president and held that position until his death in 1957.

Cornelius "Neil" Jahnke (1880–1952)

I interviewed historian Ted Perrin for information about Cornelius "Neil" Jahnke, a pioneer rancher in Saskatchewan who got his start on what used to be the American-owned Matador Ranch near Main Centre, along the South Saskatchewan River. According to Ted, over the winter of 1906–07, the Matador Ranch lost about half the fresh cattle they'd imported the previous year, half of which were two-year-olds and the other half three-year-olds. In the spring of 1907, Cornelius skinned the hides off many of these dead cattle (it's not known how many), which he found in coulees. He then sold the hides for $10 apiece and used the money he earned to buy his own ranch. His four sons—Ben, Peter, Elmer and Bruce—also had their own ranches and were pioneer ranchers in their own way. After the Matador Ranch was dissolved, the Jahnke family ran about 4500 cattle on what later became Matador Community Pasture between 1923 and 1951. They had their own field, which became known as "Jahnke Field" by locals in the area.

Andy Russell (1915–2005)

Andrew G.A. "Andy" Russell was a well-known Canadian big-game guide, outfitter, author, photographer, filmmaker, rancher, conservationist and environmentalist. He devoted his life to the protection of wildlife and wildlife habitat, especially grizzly bears. In recognition of his environmental advocacy, he received honorary degrees from the University of Lethbridge, the University of Calgary and the University of Alberta. In 1976, he received the Julian T. Crandall Award for his efforts in conservation, and in 1977, he was honored with the Order of Canada. He received an Alberta Order of Bighorn Award, Alberta's highest conservation award, in 2002. Andy Russell was a celebrity icon among Canada's conservation community and at heart a genuine throwback to Alberta's pioneer ranchers and horsemen.

DID YOU  KNOW?

Andy Russell's summer home was called Hawk's Nest and was located in the narrow belt of foothills to the east of the majestic Alberta Rockies in southwestern Alberta. The home afforded an inspirational, panoramic view of the land he dearly loved with a view of Alberta's prairies and the imposing Chief Mountain on the southern horizon. He wrote 12 books, among them *The Canadian Cowboy: Stories of Cows, Cowboys and Cayuses* (1995).

Cecil Chase (1917–?)

Cecil Chase is a member of the BC Cowboy Hall of Fame and according to their archives "represents one of the finest examples of the living pioneer spirit in the province of BC." Born in Chase, British Columbia, on April 1, 1917, Cecil developed a lifelong commitment to the pioneer and cowboy spirit. In the 1960s, he made a name for himself as a tamer of wild horses.

He worked as a cowboy, logger and mill worker, and during the 1970s and '80s, he ran cattle on his leased property, which was located on Neskonlith Lake, near Chase.

DID YOU  KNOW?

The village of Chase was named after Cecil's grandfather, Whitfield Chase, who purchased the land from the government.

R.M. "Red" Allison (1926–)

According to the BC Cowboy Hall of Fame, Red Allison has "a deep-rooted history in the pioneer cowboy and ranching industry." Allison was born in Kamloops and grew up in the area that is now known as Tranquille and North Kamloops. Later on, he worked for the Harper Ranch and 57 Mile Ranch and spent a short stint in the army. Subsequently, he worked for Henry Cornwall at Cherry Creek, then at the Alkali Lake Ranch, the Circle S, the Gang Ranch, Tranquille Farm, Fintry Estate and, finally, in 1960, he bought the Riske Creek Store. He was a founding member of the Interior Rodeo Association and presently contracts timed-event stock for the BC Rodeo Association and jackpot rodeos in the Interior.

William "Bill" Twan (1913–88)

One of 12 children, Bill Twan was born in Alexandria, British Columbia. At the age of 13, he quit school and went to work as both manager and cowboss for the Alkali Lake Ranch, where he spent most of his life. He ran a cowboy crew of up to 20, maintained the herd and oversaw the range. Twan's skill with horses and cattle was apparently well known throughout Cariboo Country. To his tribute, his ability to train horses was obvious in the cutting work shown by the horses that he rode day to day. A 1950s CBC documentary called *The Lazy Cross* (named after the ranch brand) was mostly focused on Bill working cattle. He also raced horses and competed in roping, riding, Roman racing and chariot racing. In the late 1940s and early 1950s, he was a regular winner in stake and Roman races. A cowboy to the end of his life, he always said, "You are no kind of cowboy at all if you ever look after yourself before your horse at the end of the day."

Oliver Loving (1812–67)

Texas cattle rancher Oliver Loving pioneered early American cattle drives with Charles Goodnight, and they jointly forged what became known as the Goodnight-Loving Trail (although it had been used previously by other cattlemen). The trail went from Texas to Fort Sumner, New Mexico, and on to Denver, Colorado, and was used to supply cattle to cavalry posts, Native American reservations and gold mines near Denver. In 1866, Loving rounded up a herd of cattle with Charles Goodnight and began the long drive to Fort Sumner, where some 8000 Navajos had been settled on the nearby Bosque Redondo Reservation. Loving was mortally wounded by Comaches on a later cattle drive and died of gangrene on September 25, 1867.

DID YOU  KNOW?

Oliver Loving has been inducted into the National Cowboy Hall of Fame in Oklahoma City, Oklahoma. In addition to Loving County in Texas, the village of Loving, New Mexico, is named in his honor.

John Simpson Chisum (1824–84)

Born in Hardeman County, Tennessee, John Chisum was a wealthy American cattle baron and pioneer Texas cattleman.

Chisum started ranching cattle in 1854 and was one of the first ranchers to drive his cattle to New Mexico to supply U.S. Cavalry posts and Native American reservations. During the Civil War, Chisum supplied beef to the Confederate troops west of the Mississippi. He blazed the historic Chisum Trail from Paris, Texas, to New Mexico circa 1867.

Chisum later bought land along the Pecos River and became the owner of a large ranch with over 100,000 head of cattle, though he lost thousands of cattle to rustlers. He was a major figure in the southwestern cattle industry for nearly 30 years, most of which were spent in Texas. Unusual for a rancher, Chisum was also a cattle dealer and spent much of his time looking for new markets. When he died, his estate was worth half a million dollars, a fortune at the time.

DID YOU  KNOW?

Chisum and the story of his life have been portrayed on film. Some of the prominent performers to play John Chisum include John Wayne in *Chisum* (1970) and James Coburn in *Young Guns II* (1990).

Charles Goodnight (1836–1929)

Charles "Charlie" Goodnight was perhaps the best-known rancher in Texas in his day. He is sometimes known as the "father of the Texas Panhandle." According to *From Ranch to Railhead with Charles Goodnight* by Deborah Hedstrom-Page, essayist and historian J. Frank Dobie said that Goodnight "approached greatness more nearly than any other cowman of history." He was born on the family farm in Macoupin County, Illinois, and moved to Texas in 1845 with his mother and stepfather. Along with Oliver Loving, he laid out a cattle drive route in 1866 from Texas to New Mexico, which became known as the Goodnight-Loving Trail, one of the Southwest's most heavily used cattle trails. In 1876, he founded the JA Ranch, the first in the Texas Panhandle.

DID YOU  KNOW?

Charles Goodnight is credited with assembling the first chuckwagon.

James Butler "Wild Bill" Hickok (1837–76)

James Butler Hickok, better known as Wild Bill Hickok, was one of America's most notorious gunfighters and gamblers. He goes down in history as a dashing frontiersman, army scout and lawman who reputedly helped bring law and order to the frontier West. Hickok was a long-time friend of Buffalo Bill Cody, whom he protected from being beaten when Cody was just 11 years old.

Wild Bill's iconic status is rooted in a shootout that took place in July 1861 in Rock Creek, Nebraska, and came to be known as the McCanles Massacre. One report claims that the incident began when David McCanles, along with some members of his family and several other members of his Confederate gang, came to the Pony Express Rock Creek Station demanding payment for a property that had been bought from him. Hickok, a stablehand at the time, allegedly killed six men despite being severely injured himself. Although there have been other versions of this incident, the initial publicity garnered Hickok celebrity status back in the day. Press reports escalated after he was romantically linked to Martha Jane Cannary, also known as "Calamity Jane," who was famous for her riding and shooting skills.

Wild Bill Hickok, 1837

On August 2, 1876, Hickok was shot from behind and killed while playing poker in a saloon in Deadwood, Dakota Territory (now South Dakota), by an unsuccessful gambler. The card hand he held at the time of his death—a pair of black aces and a pair of black eights—has come to be known in poker as the "Dead Man's Hand."

DID YOU  **KNOW?**

In 1979, Wild Bill Hickok was inducted into the Poker Hall of Fame.

Jerry Potts, scout and interpreter for the NWMP

Jerry Potts (1840–96)

Of Anglo-Métis heritage, Jerry Potts was a celebrated Canadian frontier hero. He was born in Montana and went on to become a renowned buffalo hunter, horse trader, interpreter and scout. Potts remained close to his mother's Kainai culture and could speak several Aboriginal languages. He achieved renown in Canada as a scout for the storied North-West Mounted Police, who hired him in September 1874 as a guide, interpreter and scout. His contract as an NWMP guide lasted 22 years, and his work earned him the rank of special constable. He chose the location for the first North-West Mounted Police post, Fort Macleod, located in southern Alberta.

The pain of throat cancer forced Potts to retire at age 58, and he died a year later, on July 14, 1896, at Fort Macleod. He was buried there with full honors for his time with the NWMP.

DID YOU  KNOW?

By the time Potts was 25, he was a wealthy man for his day largely because of his success as a horse trader. His herd averaged about 100 horses, which made him the second wealthiest person (by Native American standards) in Montana, wealth being measured by the Plains people in terms of the number of horses a man owned.

AWESOME

A 1912 painting, *Single-Handed*, by famed American artist Charles Marion Russell, features a lone mounted policeman attempting to arrest a Blood (one of the Blackfoot Nations) warrior, most likely in Canada. Though the relationship between the police and the Blackfoot was largely peaceful, the North-West Mounted Police imposed laws on the Blackfoot (such as no raiding other tribes) that they found restrictive and hard to understand.

COWGIRLS

There have been several celebrated cowgirls known for their marksmanship and riding accomplishments—some perhaps more for their notoriety as folk criminals during the settlement of the early West. In more recent times, some have become known for their pursuit of noble worldly causes. The most famous cowgirl Wild West performers will be covered elsewhere in this book.

Calamity Jane, circa 1901

Martha "Calamity Jane" Cannary (1852–1903)

Portrayed in photographs as being a no-nonsense woman, Martha Jane Cannary is best known by her nickname "Calamity Jane." She was an American frontierswoman and a professional scout, but gained notoriety as an acquaintance of Wild Bill Hickok. She became famous fighting in the

Indian Wars as a scout for General George A. Custer at Fort Russell in Wyoming Territory.

Calamity Jane was born in Princeton, Missouri, and as a child she enjoyed being in the outdoors, was fond of nature and had an early and abiding interest in horses. In her writings, she says she began riding at an early age, becoming an expert rider with the ability "to ride the most vicious and stubborn of horses." She was fond of dressing in men's clothing and had a reputation for swearing and being a hard drinker. Later in life, she became an alcoholic and, her reputation badly tarnished, worked on and off as a prostitute.

Calamity Jane dictated tales of her life on the frontier in an autobiographical booklet in 1896, which some historians claim is not completely factual. The booklet had highly mixed reviews, and some portrayed her as nothing more than a charlatan "prone to outrageous behavior."

DID YOU  KNOW?

Martha Jane Cannary was involved in several campaigns in the long-running military conflicts with Native Americans on the American frontier. Her unconfirmed claim was that: "It was during this campaign [in 1872–73] that I was christened Calamity Jane." This event allegedly took place in Goose Creek, Wyoming (the present-day town of Sheridan), where an officer named Captain Egan was in command of the post. Egan was injured during an ambush by Native Americans, and Martha Jane Cannary rode to his aid and rescued him as he was about to fall from his saddle. According to Martha Jane, upon recovering, Captain Egan reportedly said, "I name you Calamity Jane, the heroine of the plains," a nickname she bore for the rest of her life.

Jane McWha Fortune (1838–1918)

Kamloops rancher Jane McWha Fortune worked with her husband William on their Tranquille Ranch near Kamloops, British Columbia. She's a fitting example of a tough Canadian woman who became a local legend because of her determination and perseverance. She wasn't one to suffer fools gladly and pushed John Mara, a local member of Parliament and a Kamloops entrepreneur, off a steamer when the two were crossing Kamloops Lake because Mara had the audacity to disagree with her. On another occasion, she boxed the ears of an Aboriginal man she caught stealing potatoes. Oddly, she was best known as "Lady Jane" and was renowned for her excellent cooking and her business abilities, as well as for her determination and boldness. She was the couple's business manager and an equal partner in running the ranch, which flourished under her guidance.

DID YOU  KNOW?

Jane McWha Fortune stared down a local miner in 1910 after he angered her, then chased him when he ran off. She caught up with him when he ran into a stream, grabbed him by the collar and dragged him to shore. Nobody knows what happened next, but forever afterward she was respectfully called "Lady Jane."

 COWBOY WISDOM

"When you're throwin' your weight around, be ready to have it thrown around by somebody else."

Lucille Mulhall (1885–1940)

Known as the original cowgirl, Lucille Mulhall was born in St. Louis, Missouri, and was raised on her family's Mulhall Ranch in Oklahoma Territory (near the present-day town of Mulhall). One of the first women to compete with men in roping and riding events, she was known variously as "Rodeo Queen," "Queen of the Western Prairie" and "Queen of the Saddle." She performed in many rodeo and Wild West shows throughout her career and was a star in the Miller Brothers 101 Ranch Wild West Show before going on to form her own troupe in 1913. In 1916, she produced her own rodeo, Lucille Mulhall's Roundup. She was inducted into the American Rodeo Hall of Fame in 1975 and the National Cowgirl Hall of Fame in 1977.

DID YOU  KNOW?

Lucille Mulhall is celebrated as the first American cowgirl, an appellation bestowed by Teddy Roosevelt after seeing her ride at the Mulhall Ranch. As the story goes, Roosevelt told her that if she could rope a wolf, he would invite her to his inaugural parade. She came back three hours later dragging a dead wolf behind her.

Connie Douglas Reeves (1901–2003)

Born in Eagle Pass, Texas, Connie Reeves was one of the first women to study law at a Texas law school. Reeves taught high school in San Antonio, Texas, and started working part-time as a riding instructor at Camp Waldemar, a summer camp in Hunt, Texas, in 1936. She was a riding instructor at the camp for 67 years, and it's estimated that she taught 30,000 girls how to ride—a remarkable achievement. She became the oldest member of the National Cowgirl

Museum and Hall of Fame and was elected to the Cowgirl Hall of Fame in 1997. Reeves rode in the parade to honor the Cowgirl Hall of Fame when it moved to new headquarters in Fort Worth in 2002; she was over 100 years old at the time. A full-size statue of Connie Reeves stands on the stable grounds at Camp Waldemar.

DID YOU KNOW?

Connie Reeves died of cardiac arrest in San Antonio on August 17, 2003, which was 12 days after she was thrown from her horse, Dr. Pepper. She was 101 years old. Her motto was, "Always saddle your own horse."

Dale Evans (1912–2001)

The one and only long-standing cowgirl Hollywood star was Dale Evans, an American writer, movie star and singer-songwriter. Born Lucille Wood Smith in Uvalde, Texas, she took the name Dale Evans in the early 1930s to promote her singing career. Her clean-cut public life was in direct contrast to her early personal life—she eloped at age 14 and bore her first child when she was just 15. Evans was the third wife of singing cowboy Roy Rogers, whom she married in 1947—her fourth marriage and his third. From 1951 to 1957, the couple starred in the highly successful TV series *The Roy Rogers Show*, in which they continued their cowboy and cowgirl roles, with Evans riding her beloved buckskin horse, Buttermilk. Rogers and Evans were a team both on and off screen from 1946 until Rogers' death in 1998.

DID YOU KNOW?

The song "Happy Trails to You," released in 1952 and sung by Rogers and Evans, is one of the most recognized western songs ever recorded. It was the theme song for both their 1940s and 1950s radio program and their 1950s television show.

Other Famous Cowgirls

Some of Hollywood's most memorable cowgirls include the adorable Doris Day and the voluptuous Jane Russell and Raquel Welch. Aside from being three of the biggest names in Hollywood, they all donned the cowgirl costume for a few movies, as did Jane Fonda and Elizabeth Montgomery. In the 1953 musical comedy *Calamity Jane*, Doris Day played the title role alongside Howard Keel as Wild Bill Hickok. Jane Fonda starred in the title role in the 1965 comedy western *Cat Ballou*, as a schoolteacher who becomes an outlaw when she returns home to discover that the Wolf City Development Corporation wants to take the family ranch away from her father. The opening scene featuring a drunken gunfighter, Kid Shelleen (Lee Marvin), who Cat Ballou (Jane Fonda) hires to help defend the ranch, is hilarious and worth the price of admission to the movie in itself.

WHERE COWBOYS HANG THEIR HATS

There are several provinces and states that are considered all-around cowboy places. In Canada, Alberta would top the list, loosely followed by British Columbia and Saskatchewan. Interestingly, there is also a strong following of cowboys and rodeos in the province of Quebec, despite the fact that it is in eastern Canada, outside the traditional Wild West. The western states of Arizona, California, Colorado, Idaho, Oklahoma, Montana, Nevada, New Mexico, Texas and Utah are all considered "cowboy places," and to a lesser degree Kansas, Oregon and Washington. Travel specialist Terry Baldwin has written about what he considers to be the top cowboy towns in the United States where you might want to hang your hat and stretch your legs. Most of these western towns are associated with cowboy places.

Cowboy Canada

In Canada, there are fewer towns and cities renowned for their western heritage than in the United States. The most notable Canadian center would be Calgary, home of the world-famous Calgary Stampede, and nearby Cochrane, a short distance to the west of Calgary, nestled in the picturesque foothills of the majestic Alberta Rockies.

DID YOU KNOW?

Set in the rolling foothills of the Canadian Rockies, the Bar U Ranch is the only National Historic Site in Canada to commemorate the history and importance of ranching.

The site has many historic buildings and structures that illustrate various stages of ranching development and is rich in cultural landscape features. A visitor orientation center and a vibrant living history program interpret a time when the West was young on the Canadian range.

Downtown Calgary with the renowned Saddledome in the foreground

Calgary, Alberta

Calgary, often affectionately called "Cowtown," is the largest city in Alberta and is set on the edge of the foothills of Alberta's Rocky Mountains and the sweeping prairie to the east. Although a cosmopolitan city, Calgary is proud of its cowboy roots and boasts the world-renowned Calgary Stampede, an annual rodeo, exhibition and festival held every July. The 10-day event, which bills itself as "the Greatest Outdoor Show on Earth," attracts over one million visitors per year from around the world. It features one of the world's largest rodeos, a parade, midway, concerts and stage shows, agricultural competitions, chuckwagon racing and exhibitions by First Nations groups.

Calgary's White Hats

The Cowtown equivalent of offering the keys to the city, the tradition of "white-hatting" dates back to the 1950s. The newest generation of royalty, the Duke and Duchess of Cambridge, Will and Kate, were officially welcomed to Calgary with a White Hat Ceremony on July 8, 2011, by Mayor Naheed Nenshi. Brian Hanson, vice-president of Smithbilt Hats, handcrafted the headgear that greeted the Duke and Duchess.

The company produces three styles of white hats:

- The New West, made of glazed canvas, sells for $18.50 and Smithbilt recommends it for large groups who need to be Stampede-ready.

- The Old West model is made of merino wool and is priced at $72.50.

- The Cadillac of Smithbilt hats is the Wild West, the "Official White Hat," and is made of 100 percent rabbit fur. It retails at $199.99.

Cochrane Ranche House

The Cochrane Ranche House, formally known as the Western Heritage Centre, officially opened in June 2004. The origins of the center date to 1985, when two founding groups, the Stockmen's Memorial Foundation and the Canadian Rodeo Historical Association, came together to preserve the Ranche House as a historical center. The spirit of cowboys is fairly palpable in this storied attraction.

Longview, Alberta

Longview is a tiny village in southwestern Alberta, located in the foothills of the Canadian Rockies, smack on the Cowboy Trail, 39 miles (64 kilometers) south of Calgary.

The flood-prone Highwood River flows west of the village. Celebrated Canadian cowboy singer Ian Tyson lives on a nearby ranch and plays the occasional concert in the local bar of the Twin Cities Hotel. Longview is a must-stop for its famed beef jerky.

DID YOU  **KNOW?**

Clint Eastwood's Academy Award–winning film *Unforgiven* was filmed in and around Longview in 1991, as was the 2003 television film *Monte Walsh*, which stars Tom Selleck.

Downtown Kamloops viewed from the surrounding hills

Kamloops, British Columbia

The city of Kamloops is located in south-central BC, at the confluence of the two branches of the Thompson River near Kamloops Lake. It can be a veritable furnace during the heat of the summer and is one of the hottest places in Canada.

Kamloops is located in the heart of BC cattle ranching country and is rich in cowboy history. Some of the BC Cowboy Hall of Fame inductees are honored at the BC Cowboy Heritage Festival in the city in May each year.

DID YOU KNOW?

The Kamloops Cowboys were a senior amateur hockey team based in Kamloops. They played in the Cariboo Hockey League from 1978 to 1979.

Williams Lake, British Columbia

Williams Lake is located in central BC on the north shore of a lake of the same name. Historic sites around Williams Lake showcase the struggles of the early settlers, the heyday of the area's gold rush and the romance of pioneering cowboys. The city is home to the Museum of the Cariboo Chilcotin, billed as a "true cowboy museum," which features photos, biographies and memorabilia of BC's outstanding cowboys and cowgirls. Williams Lake is also home to the BC Cowboy Hall of Fame, which was founded in 1998 by the BC Cowboy Heritage Society and the Museum of the Cariboo Chilcotin. In conjunction with the BC Cowboy Heritage Society, the museum also administers the nomination side of the BC Cowboy Hall of Fame.

DID YOU KNOW?

British Columbia's ranching industry spans two centuries and is older than the province! Cattlemen and cowboys truly won the West, and the Museum of the Cariboo Chilcotin is dedicated to preserving and promoting this ranching heritage.

It is the only museum in BC to focus on ranching and rodeo, and it honors the cowboys of both the past and the present.

Val Marie, Saskatchewan

The village of Val Marie ("Valley of Mary") is located in southwestern Saskatchewan just a few miles from the Canada-U.S. border. Founded in 1910 by Father Passaplan, Louis Denniel and brothers François and Léon Pinel, the settlement stands out for its ranching and cowboy history. However, as in many rural communities across western Canada, falling grain and cattle prices have caused major downturns in the local economy, resulting in population declines. Fortunately, the West Block of Grasslands National Park, which lies 6 miles (10 kilometers) east of Val Marie, attracts some tourism to the area. Grasslands National Park is the only place in Canada where the endangered black-tailed prairie dog can be found, and in 2006, plains bison were re-introduced into the park.

DID YOU KNOW?

John Palliser led the first expedition (1857–60) to explore and survey western Canada, including the area around Val Marie, to assess possible routes for the Canadian Pacific Railway and evaluate the suitability of the area for agriculture. The Palliser expedition was in many ways comparable to the Lewis and Clark expedition (1804–06) of the American West. Palliser reported that the area was dismally dry, prone to drought and unfit for habitation.

Mankota, Saskatchewan

This southern Saskatchewan village is located about 93 miles (150 kilometers) southeast of the city of Swift Current. It is home to the Mankota Stockmen's Weigh Co. Ltd. and is in the heart of cattle country in southwestern Saskatchewan. The Mankota Stockyards hold cow sales every Friday throughout the year, and the village's motto is "We are Proud of our cattle, Proud of our Market." There is also an annual rodeo, held in May, at the Mankota Rodeo Grounds.

DID YOU  KNOW?

Mankato as a boy's name is of Native American origin and means "blue earth."

Maple Creek, Saskatchewan

The town of Maple Creek is located in southwestern Saskatchewan and is known as the community "Where past is present." Each autumn, the town hosts the Maple Creek Cowboy Poetry Gathering and Western Art and Gear Show. Billed as "a rich tapestry of music, art, and especially poetry...of the cowboy and of the West," the three-day Maple Creek Cowboy Poetry Gathering started in 1989 and was the creation of Doris Bircham and Kim Taylor. People come from all over to attend this long-standing festival to participate and take in the cowboy poetry atmosphere.

DID YOU KNOW?

It wasn't until after the North-West Mounted Police established Fort Walsh in 1875 that people began to settle in the Cypress Hills around Maple Creek. At the time, Fort Walsh became the most important, the largest and the most heavily armed NWMP post.

DID YOU KNOW?

Cowboy places and namesakes are synonymous with the brand names of many cars and trucks: Bronco, Mustang, Longhorn, Cheyenne, Laramie, Laredo, Montana, Santa Fe and Dakota.

Allen Street, Tombstone, Arizona

Tombstone, Arizona

This historic western city in Cochise County, Arizona, was founded in 1879 by scout and prospector Ed Schieffelin in what was then Pima County, Arizona Territory. It was one of the last wide-open frontier boomtowns in the Old West and is best known for being the location of the gunfight at the OK Corral. Known as "The Town Too Tough to Die," its present-day motto, it draws most of its revenue from tourism. From its founding in 1879, shortly after silver was discovered there, the population grew quickly, as did the crime rate. Things got so bad so fast that President Chester A. Arthur declared martial law and sent troops to calm the locals down. These days, visitors to the cowboy town of 1500 exceed 450,000 yearly to partake in its western heritage.

DID YOU KNOW?

Within two years of its founding in 1879, Tombstone had four churches, two banks, three newspapers, a school, a bowling alley, an icehouse and an ice cream parlor, as well as 110 saloons, 14 gambling halls and numerous dance halls and brothels.

Boot Hill Museum, Dodge City, Kansas

Dodge City, Kansas

The town of Dodge City can trace its origins to 1871, when rancher Henry J. Sitler built a sod house west of Fort Dodge to oversee his cattle operations in the region. Named after the nearby fort, Dodge City is famous for its history as a wild frontier town of the Old West. Its storied and often seedy past is documented and displayed for visitors in the Boot Hill Museum and Front Street. Additionally, the Santa Fe Trail, Fort Dodge and the Gunfighters Wax Museum are listed as must-see attractions.

DID YOU KNOW?

Although many towns have cemeteries with the name "Boot Hill," the first one was in Dodge City. In the Old West, the moniker was popular for the graveyards of gunfighters and others who "died with their boots on."

Miles City, Montana

Miles City, the county seat of Custer County, Montana, was once home to Butch Cassidy and Teddy Roosevelt. Founded in 1877, this eastern Montana town grew out of a tavern and was named after General Nelson A. Miles. A veteran of the American Civil War, the Indian Wars and the Spanish-American War, Miles is credited for effectively bringing what remained of the native Plains people into subjugation during the last decade of the 1800s. The biggest attractions in Miles City include the Range Riders Museum, the Cowtown Beef Breeders Show and the Bucking Horse Sale.

DID YOU KNOW?

Livestock speculators brought thousands of cattle to the open ranges near Miles City in the late 1880s. The railroad was extended through the area, and Texas ranchers drove cattle to Miles City to fatten them on free grass and move them to where they could be loaded on trains bound for slaughterhouses in Chicago.

Elko, Nevada

Elko boasts a population of just over 15,000 today. Besides featuring a western way of life, the city is know for the National Cowboy Poetry Gathering, while several museums in the city connect visitors with the cowboy way of life. Elko is also home to the Western Folklife Center.

DID YOU KNOW?

Prostitution is legal in Elko, and the town hosts a number of active brothels. Under Nevada law, any county with a population of less than 400,000 is allowed to license brothels if it so chooses.

Oklahoma City, Oklahoma

One of only two American capital cities with their state name as part of the city name, Oklahoma City boasted a population of 600,000 in 2012. The name Oklahoma means "land of the red people" in the Choctaw language. Despite its large population, it still ranks as a key cowboy town because it is where the National Cowboy and Western Heritage Museum is located, and the city is also billed as the "Horse Show Capital of the World." Even though it's a city by name, there's no denying it's a cowboy town at heart. Over the course of the year, activities include the annual Chuck Wagon Gathering and Children's Cowboy Festival, the Western Heritage Awards and plenty of rodeos. Oklahoma City also features one of the largest livestock markets in the world.

DID YOU KNOW?

Oklahoma City was settled by the historic Land Run of April 22, 1889, and the city's population grew to more than 10,000 in a single day. Those who sneaked over the boundaries the night before the Land Run to claim the area around Oklahoma City were known as "Sooners."

Deadwood, South Dakota, circa 1890

Deadwood, South Dakota

Located in western South Dakota's Black Hills, Deadwood was named for the dead trees found in its gulch. The legendary Wyatt Earp, Seth Bullock, Wild Bill Hickok and Calamity Jane, names that are synonymous with the Old West, all have ties to Deadwood. According to the town's website, Deadwood is where "Wild Bill Hickok's luck ran out, but yours begins," a hook to its present-day gambling halls. The town's website advertises that "with over 80 historic gaming halls and year-round wild events, you can play the night away." Founded in 1876, the former gold rush town of about 1300 is on the rebound, thanks in part to the legalization of gambling in 1989. However, long before its modern-day gaming halls were built, Deadwood had a reputation for being a lawless town run by gamblers and gunslingers.

Seth Bullock was a sheriff, hardware store owner and U.S. marshal. When he was appointed sheriff, one of his first duties was to confront Dodge City deputy marshal Wyatt Earp, who was supposedly interested in the sheriff's job. Bullock told Earp that his services were not needed, and a week later, Earp left Deadwood to return to Dodge City.

County courthouse, Bandera, Texas

Bandera, Texas

Bandera, in Texas Hill Country, calls itself the "Cowboy Capital of the World," a title that originated when it became a staging area for the great cattle drives back in the day. This small town, with a population just over 1200, is home to the Frontier Times Museum, and dude ranches are an important part of the local economy.

DID YOU  KNOW?

In confirmation of Bandera as the "Cowboy Capital of the World," there's a bronze monument on the courthouse lawn that honors the many National Rodeo champions who call Bandera home.

Sheridan, Wyoming

Fort Phil Kearney, near Sheridan, Wyoming

The state of Wyoming and cowboys are synonymous. Wyoming even features a cowboy on its license plate. The north-central Wyoming town of Sheridan, with its population of about 17,000, boasts a true cowboy spirit. The Little Bighorn Battlefield National Monument is nearby, as well as Fort Phil Kearny, a state historic site. The fort was an outpost of the U.S. Army in the late 1860s along the Bozeman Trail. Sheridan's western history is revisited annually with the Sagebrush Cowboy Gathering, Buffalo Bill Days, Bozeman Trail Days and several rodeos in between.

DID YOU  **KNOW?**

Sheridan was named after General Philip Sheridan, a Union cavalry leader during the Civil War. The city is also only a short distance away from the site of the Battle of the Little Bighorn, in which General George Armstrong Custer was killed.

FRONTIER FOOD

Lean and Mean

Back in the day, cowboys lived pretty frugal lives. If they had one thing in common, it would be that they were usually lean and wiry. Actually, even by today's standards, an overweight cowboy would be an oddity. According to *Beyond the Range: A History of the Saskatchewan Stock Growers Association* (1988) by Boyd M. Anderson: "The usual roundup or trail fare was fresh beef, canned vegetables, beans, coffee, rice, macaroni, cheese and dried fruit—no butter, no potatoes except in cold weather."

Typical trail grub, 1939

Trail Fare

On the trail, cowboys would eat trail biscuits or flatbread made from dough that had been put into a pan over a camp-fire, and then covered with some glowing coals for about 15 minutes. The unleavened dough was made of flour and water, seasoned with a little salt and then rolled flat.

Canned bacon and beans were also typical grub because they were easy to prepare, along with coffee perked in an old coffeepot covered with soot, or simply an old can with a wire handle. Cowboys would eat dried beef or pork, and occasionally fresh venison when handy because it was difficult to store meat while on the trail. They might also have eggs if they were obtainable. Typically, trail grub was nothing fancy and was, for the most part, more or less just a subsistence type of diet.

A Cup of Arbuckle

Until the end of the American Civil War, coffee beans were sold green. They had to be roasted on a wood stove or in a skillet over a campfire before they could be ground and brewed. One burned bean could ruin an entire batch and quality was inconsistent. In 1865, John Arbuckle and his brother Charles, partners in a Pittsburgh grocery business, revolutionized the coffee trade by patenting a process for roasting and coating coffee beans with an egg and sugar glaze to seal in the flavor and aroma. The Arbuckles also invented a machine that efficiently roasted, ground and packaged coffee into small bags for mass distribution throughout the country.

DID YOU  KNOW?

Arbuckle's was the most popular brand of coffee following the Civil War and became a favorite in the Old West. Their Ariosa Blend became so popular that most cowboys probably didn't even know that any other coffee brand existed. Arbuckle's Coffee was prominent in such notorious cow towns as Dodge City and Tombstone. To many older cowboys, Arbuckle's Ariosa Blend is still known as the original cowboy coffee.

Modern Grub

Meals on contemporary ranches tend to fall into the "filling" category because of the amount of physical work required for day-to-day activities. Most ranchers work hard outdoors during the day, burning up a lot of calories.

For breakfast, ham, sausages or bacon and eggs would be the norm, with toast and jam, steaming hot coffee—something filling to start off the day. Lunch would likewise be nutritious, and depending on the time of day, might be quite similar to what would be served for dinner. Fried or roast chicken, ribs, steaks and roasts would all be standard fare for the main course, along with baked or mashed potatoes, thick gravy, steamed carrots, green or yellow beans, and often homemade bread or buns.

Chutney and homemade pickles—pickled beets or carrots or bread-and-butter pickles—are common on farms and ranches. Stews, meatloaf, casseroles, baked ham, scalloped potatoes, yams and parsnips might also be regular items. Baked beans would likely be somewhat rare on most ranches these days but remain a fixture nonetheless. A common feature on many cattlemen's kitchen (or dining room) tables would be a rotating turntable so that all the fixings would be within easy reach of everyone.

DID YOU KNOW?

Chuckwagons were essentially mobile kitchens containing food, supplies and cooking utensils. Camp cooks often used Dutch ovens to prepare food over an open fire.

CHUCKWAGONS: KITCHENS ON WHEELS

A camp cook and his chuckwagon near Marfa, Texas, 1939

The Groanin' Cart

The invention of the chuckwagon is attributed to Charles Goodnight, a prominent Texas rancher who introduced the concept of a mobile kitchen in 1866. Often called *the* original "Meals on Wheels," back in the day, cowboys sometimes called a well-loaded chuckwagon the "groanin' cart."

To make the chuckwagon, Goodnight modified an army-surplus wagon by building shelves, drawers and cubbyholes behind a hinged lid that lowered to become a worktable for the cook. The device was first used in 1866 on the inaugural cattle drive on what would become the Goodnight-Loving Trail from Texas to New Mexico and Colorado. Chuckwagons were an integral part of early cattle drives and went on to become a veritable institution in their day.

A Mess of Food

The role of both the chuckwagon and the cook is covered in *Beyond the Range: A History of the Saskatchewan Stock Growers Association* (1988) by Boyd M. Anderson. A mess box, also called a "chuck box," was bolted on the back of the chuckwagon. The door to the mess box was hinged on the back of the wagon and formed a table for the cook when it was lowered. A cookstove of heavy sheet iron with no legs was put up near the table to prepare meals. The dishes and food were put on the table for the cowboys to help themselves.

DID YOU  KNOW?

The cook was an important part of all cattle drives and drove the chuckwagon. On the trail, cowboys were paid $30 to $40 per month, whereas the cook got $50 per month, testament to his importance.

Sourdough

In the United States, sourdough was a staple, and cooks apparently jealously guarded their precious dough keg. Besides biscuits and flapjacks, the sourdough base was even sometimes used as a poultice on burns and wounds. If maintained properly, a cook's sourdough starter could last for many years.

Eating on the road during a Texas roundup, circa 1900

Beans and Brains

One of the staples in an American cowboy's diet was red Mexican beans, which were called *frijoles*, "whistle berries" or "Mexican strawberries." Rice was called "moonshine." When a guest brought food with him, he was said to bring "pot luck." "Son-of-a-gun stew" a favorite cowboy dish, was made of cow brains, sweetbreads and choice pieces of a freshly killed calf. In making this stew, the camp cook was said to "throw everything in the pot but the horns and hide." When fuel was scarce, the cook resorted to using "cow chips" (dried cow droppings) instead of wood for cooking.

Dinnertime!

Some of the familiar calls of the camp cook might be the following:

- "Here it is, come an' get it!"
- "Roll out, roll out while she's hot!"
- "Boneheads, boneheads, take it away!"

DID YOU  KNOW?

The term "chuckwagon" comes from "chuck," an unpoetic slang term for food, and not from the nickname for Charles. The chuckwagon was designated the official vehicle of Texas in 2003.

American Chuckwagon Association

Dedicated to preserving chuckwagon heritage, the American Chuckwagon Association sponsors a number of competitive "cook-offs" throughout the United States. Competitors are judged on the authenticity of their wagon and utensils, and on the quality of their food, which is scored in five categories: meat, potatoes, beans, bread and dessert.

COOKBOOKS AND RECIPES

Country Cookbooks

There's no shortage of cowboy cookbooks and recipes on the market, and they are featured in many countries from Canada and the United States to Australia. Not only are there cowboy cookbooks from various countries around the world, but there are also many that feature recipes from various provinces, states and even families and ranches.

Good Food for Hard-working Cowboys

If I've learned one thing from talking to women on various farms and ranches in Alberta, it's that country women do not like recipes that call for ingredients they don't have in their kitchens. A second thing I've learned is that country women are usually terrific cooks, and they'll have you coming back for seconds and even thirds. If you've ever done a hard day's labor pitching bales of hay, tossing stooks of grain into a threshing machine (back in the old days), building fences or branding cattle in the great outdoors, you'll work up an appetite. You'll go through a lot of calories and will be hungry at lunch or supper. Actually, on many farms and ranches the main meal is often lunch because everyone works so hard during the day.

Author's Favorite Restaurants

You might wonder if I have a favorite "western" restaurant. Actually, there are a couple—the Flying N in Claresholm, Alberta (now closed), and Borrie's, a family restaurant in Black Eagle, Montana, just north of Great Falls.

Nouveau Cowboy Cuisine

More recently, there's been a wave of "nouveau cowboy" cookbooks that feature popular recipes, such as cowboy quiche, chipotle steaks, nachos, fajitas and potato skins, all definitely with a Hispanic flare. There's a lot of regional variation in cowboy recipes in Canada and the U.S., but one thing they have in common are steaks, roasts, ribs and ground beef as main dishes. There are also cookbooks that focus on techniques, such as cooking with a Dutch (camp) oven or barbecue.

DID YOU KNOW?

Ranch dressing, the bestselling salad dressing flavor in the U.S. since 1992, originated on the Hidden Valley Guest Ranch near Santa Barbara, California. In the 1950s, the ranch owners made a dressing with herbs, spices and buttermilk that caught on with their guests. Later, the dressing was sold as a dry mix that would then be combined with buttermilk and mayonnaise or sour cream. Now, the Hidden Valley brand appears on several varieties of bottled ranch dressing in supermarkets. It's also a very popular dip for vegetables or chips.

Prairie Oysters

The term "prairie oyster" may refer to:

- Prairie Oyster, the Canadian country music band
- Rocky Mountain oysters, which are are bull calf testicles that have been deep-fried after being peeled, coated in flour, salt and pepper, and sometimes pounded flat. They're most often served as an appetizer with a cocktail sauce dip

A prairie oyster cocktail, a traditional cowboy hangover remedy, is made with a raw egg, Worcestershire sauce, hot sauce, vinegar, salt and pepper. These ingredients are combined in a glass and swallowed in one gulp.

Favorite Cookbooks

In my home province of Alberta, some of my go-to cowboy recipe books are getting a bit dog-eared. I can't say enough about the *75th 4-H Favorites* cookbook (circa 1992), which covers the gamut of western Canadian farm and ranch recipes ranging from appetizers and dips to cakes, desserts, meats, preserves and vegetables.

Another favorite is Jean Hoare's *Best Little Cookbook in the West* (1983), which features "delicious recipes and warm memories from the famous Flying N," a popular eatery in Claresholm, Alberta, sadly now closed. Their beef Wellington was to die for!

The *I Love Alberta Beef* (2004) cookbook published by the Alberta Beef Producers is loaded with outstanding recipes and is a real tribute to the province's beef industry. I can't say enough about how many terrific recipes are in this classic western cookbook.

At the farm level, the *Cross Bar Ranch Centennial Legacy Cookbook* (2010) is a "tribute to the Cross Bar cooks—past and present." It features many wonderful recipes from members of the Cross Bar Ranch family, including Cocktail Smokies, Fire-grilled Bruschetta and Beef Liver and Bacon Pie.

DID YOU KNOW?

There's even a cookbook called *Cooking the Cowboy Way: Recipes Inspired by Campfires, Chuck Wagons, and Ranch Kitchens* (2009), written by cowboy-turned-chef Grady Spears.

Pancake Breakfasts

The pancake breakfast is a local institution during the world-renowned Calgary Stampede. Dozens of these breakfasts are held daily throughout the city, hosted by community groups, corporations, churches, politicians and the Calgary Stampede itself. The tradition of pancake breakfasts dates back to the 1923 Stampede, when a chuckwagon driver by the name of Jack Morton invited passing citizens to join him for his morning meals. Typically, pancake breakfasts feature pancakes and syrup, either bacon or sausages and steaming hot coffee. Over 60,000 people might be in attendance at the largest breakfasts.

Cowboy Breakfast Recipe

There are many different cowboy breakfast recipes, but the following one is more or less typical:

Ingredients
½ lb pork sausage
1 package country-style frozen hash brown potatoes
6 eggs
1 c shredded cheddar cheese

Directions
1. Brown the sausages in a skillet.
2. Add the frozen hash browns, stirring occasionally until done.

3. Break the eggs into a bowl, whisk them, and then add them to the sausages and hash browns in the skillet. Cook until the eggs are done.

4. Sprinkle the shredded cheddar cheese over everything in the skillet and let melt.

5. Serve with steaming hot coffee and enjoy.

Baked Beans Recipe

A go-to recipe for baked beans is shown below and was taken from my award-winning *Fish & Wild Game Recipes, Volume 1* (2006) cookbook, published by Sports Scene Publications Inc. I've searched high and low for good baked beans recipes and adapted this particular one from Internet sites and various cookbooks. It is about as low-cal as you're likely to find.

Ingredients

1½ c dried beans (e.g. small white pea or navy beans, or the larger Great Northern beans)

½ Spanish onion (diced)

2 slices of bacon (chopped)

½ tsp salt

¼ tsp pepper

¼ c molasses

1 tsp dry mustard

2 tsp red wine vinegar

1 Tbsp brown sugar or maple syrup

½ c ketchup

Directions

1. Soak the beans overnight in cold water in a large cooking pot; add 3 or 4 times as much water as there are beans because the beans will swell.

2. Drain the contents the following morning and rinse the beans under cold water.

3. Cover the beans with water, bring to a boil and simmer for 30 minutes.

4. Drain the liquid in which the beans were cooked into a mixing bowl and set it aside.

5. Put the beans in a Boston bean pot. I use a pot manufactured by Medalta Potteries Ltd. of Redcliff, Alberta, that holds 5 cups. This particular recipe is geared for 5 cups of baked beans, so please don't vary the amount of ingredients or else you must adjust them to the capacity of your casserole dish.

6. Mix the seasonings in a measuring bowl (salt, pepper, mustard, brown sugar or syrup, molasses and ketchup) and pour over top of the beans.

7. Add the diced onion and bacon (you can also use salt pork or trim from a cooked ham). Stir well. Or, add the beans, onions and bacon in layers and top off with the seasonings mixture, then stir.

8. Top off the beans with the water in which the beans were cooked.

9. Bake the beans in an oven at 250°F for 6–8 hours. Periodically add extra bean water (as needed) to keep them covered. Stir occasionally.

A word of advice to stay on the right side of your better half—until you get the hang of it, place some tinfoil on a baking tray underneath the Boston bean pot to collect any juices that might boil over, as it's easier than cleaning the oven. Baked beans are a real treat any time of the year. They're so good and round off any meal of beef or venison. They can also be a meal in themselves, enjoyed with freshly baked bread topped with butter, along with a beverage of your choice.

Baked beans were a staple of chuckwagon meals.

SADDLE HORSES AND COW PONIES

A cowboy's best friend

What Makes a Good Horse?

A horse is just a horse, isn't it? Not really. Horses are like cats and dogs in that there are many different breeds used for different purposes, for example, thoroughbred racehorses. At present, no fewer than 18 horse breeds are officially recognized. Not unlike a racehorse, a well-trained saddle horse with good bloodlines is worth a small fortune. Working or stock horses are made, not born, and have to be trained to work with cattle. Also, because a rider usually needs to keep one hand free while working cattle, the horse must neck rein and have good "cow sense"—it must have an affinity for herding cattle and be able to anticipate how cattle move and react. A cowboy's horse would be his pride and joy, and to break the lonely hours on the trail, he might talk to it as though it were human.

DID YOU  KNOW?

Besides being a general and the first president of the United States, George Washington was also known as a great horseman. Thomas Jefferson apparently called him the "best horseman of the era."

The game of horseshoes

Throwing Horseshoes

Horseshoes is not a cowboy game. It is believed that camp followers of Grecian armies who could not afford a discus instead took discarded horseshoes, set up a stake and began throwing horseshoes at it. Horseshoe historians have not been able to discover when the game of quoits (throwing metal, rope or rubber rings over a set distance, usually to land over or near a spike) or horseshoes was changed so that rings or shoes rather than discuses were pitched at two stakes, but it is pretty well established that horseshoe pitching had its origin in the game of quoits and that quoits is a modification of the old Grecian game of discus throwing.

DID YOU KNOW?

The first horseshoe-pitching tournament in which competition was open to the world was held in the summer of 1910 in Bronson, Kansas. The winner was Frank Jackson, who was awarded a world championship belt with horseshoes attached to it.

Quarter Horse Origins

Nowadays, the most common ranch stock horse breed in Canada and the United States is the American quarter horse. This is one of the original American horse breeds and was developed primarily in Texas using thoroughbreds crossed with mustangs and horses of Iberian ancestry (i.e., from Spain), with an Arabian horse influence, as well as breeds from the east coast, such as the Morgan horse.

DID YOU KNOW?

The Mangalarga Marchador is a Brazilian horse breed known for having a smooth walk, canter and gallop, as well as two natural ambling gaits. Their stamina and versatility make them good stock horses. This breed was first imported into the United States in 2001, and now there are Marchador breeders and owners in many states. In 2007, the breed was introduced into Canada.

Famous Cowboy Horses

The February/March 2011 issue of *American Cowboy* magazine listed the top five greatest western movie horses and their riders:

- Trigger and Roy Rogers
- Silver and Clayton Moore (the Lone Ranger)
- Fritz and William S. Hart
- Tony and Tom Mix
- Tarzan and Ken Maynard

As an aside, Buttermilk was the name of a buckskin quarter horse mare personally owned by Roy Roger's wife, Dale Evans, and Buck was the name of a buckskin quarter horse gelding that Marshall Matt Dillon of *Gunsmoke* rode.

DID YOU KNOW?

When Trigger died in 1965, Roy Rogers arranged for the horse's hide to be stretched over a plastic likeness of a horse in a rearing position. Trigger was then put on display at the Roy Rogers–Dale Evans Museum in Branson, Missouri. Rogers also had his German shepherd, Bullet, and Dale's horse, Buttermilk, stuffed, mounted and exhibited at the museum.

Horse Sense

Part of cowboy wisdom is being able to think like
a horse—no easy task. Notable cowboy quotes that
relate to horses are listed on Rick Gore's Horsemanship
website, thinklikeahorse.org, include the following:

- "It is easier to acknowledge your horse's faults once
you have acknowledged your own."

- "Every horse, at least once in its life, deserves to be
loved by a little girl."

- "If you are riding a high horse, there ain't no way to
get down off it graceful."

- "You can have horses or you can have money, but you
can't have them both."

- "There are rules about riding a horse, but the horse
won't necessarily know them."

Know Your Horses

Cowboys classified horses into various categories:

Mustang: A wild horse

Cayuse: A wild horse from Oregon, named after the Cayuse
tribe

Bronco: A wild or semi-tame horse

Pony: A general term for a horse; used in the northwestern
U.S. in particular

Stock horses: Brood mares and their foals

Work horses: Horses harnessed to wagons and scrapers

Cutting horse: A horse trained to cut cattle out of a herd

Night horse: A sure-footed horse with good eyesight, ridden
only at night, with the ability to detect cattle in the dark

A wild mustang on the prairies

DID YOU  **KNOW?**

Night horses were the most valuable horses on cattle drives. During the night, riders would circle the herd to keep it in one spot while the other cowboys slept. Nighttime stampedes were always a big concern because cattle are relatively easy to spook when it's dark.

COWBOY LINGO

For those interested in the lowdown on cowboy lingo, there's actually a book called Cowboy Lingo *(2000) by Ramon F. Adams that features cowboy-speak and colorful cowboy terms. It's an interesting read, full of words and phrases that characterize cowboy culture. Adams also writes about many sayings that you'll recognize because they're now part of everyday language, including "blue lightning," "star gazing" and "the whole shebang." Cowboy lingo captures the living speech of the Great Plains and serves as a window into the soul of the American West and the men and women who settled the frontier. Some of the more common and colorful terms are familiar to modern folks, whereas others are rather obscure. For example, the top rail of the main corral was referred to as the "op'ra house."*

Spanglish

Early American cowboys picked up a lot of their lingo from Mexicans who lived in the West, as well as Native Americans and the French. They especially borrowed Spanish Mexican terms that applied to ranching. For example, the Spanish word *vamos* means "leave," and although cowboys revised the spelling and the pronunciation to "vamoose," they did not change the meaning. Vamoose is now a commonly used American slang word. American cowboys adopted many other Spanish words such as "lasso," "rodeo" and "amigo," which are now widely used in both Canada and the U.S.

Referring to a Ranch

"Ranch" comes from the Spanish American word *rancho*, which means "a farm," particularly one used for breeding and rearing cattle or horses. It can also refer to a cabin or a hut, or to a collection of them, in which ranchers live. There are several popular ways that ranchers might describe a ranch—as a "spread" or "outfit," for example. The owner of a ranch might be called the "presidente," "ramrod" or "big auger." The foreman was called the "top screw," "straw boss" or "cock-a-doodle-doo."

Coffee and conversation

Colloquial Cowboys

Typically, cowboys tend to speak informally. They use many contractions and frequently disregard the rules of grammar. Double negatives are very common; for example, "I haven't ever owed nothin' to no one" or "It don't mean nothin' out here." This lingo can easily be identified in country and western music and is sometimes mimicked (in jest) by other people. As the saying goes, "Imitation is the sincerest form of flattery."

DID YOU  KNOW?

Cowboys have developed and popularized many words, some of which have become part of everyday vernacular. For example, a "brand" is a mark that is burned into the skin of a cow or a horse to identify the legal owner. Nowadays, people often refer to the name of a company or product as a brand. Business people also use the word brand as a verb to describe the development of a positive and recognizable image of a product or service (i.e., to brand something).

A Cowboy Lexicon

Above board: In plain sight, without any trickery

According to Hoyle: Correct or by the book; Edward Hoyle wrote books of rules for card games, and *Hoyle's Short Treatise on the Game of Whist* included not only the rules, but gave many insights into how to win at the game

Ace in the hole: A hideout or a hidden gun; the phrase originates from the game of poker, in which a card dealt face down and kept hidden is called a "hole card," the "key card" being the ace

Arbuckle's: Coffee; taken from Arbuckle's, a popular coffee brand that was established in 1865

Balderdash: Something completely untrue or very stupid; utter nonsense, foolishness

Ballyhoo: Noisy shouting or an uproar; also sales talk, advertising or exaggeration

Bee in your bonnet: An old English phrase alluding to the state of agitation you would experience if you found a bee inside your bonnet; in cowboy-speak, it means a new idea or fixation on something

Bonanza: The discovery of an exceptionally rich vein of gold or silver or gold nuggets

Boot-licker: The equivalent of an ass-kisser or suck-up

Caboodle: The whole thing, everything; also "kit and caboodle"

Calico queen: One of many endearing terms for a prostitute

Cash in: To die; to figuratively cash in your chips at the end of your life

Cowpuncher: Cowboy; originally applied only to the chaperones of cattle shipments; usually shortened to "puncher"

Critter: Cow

Dead as a door nail: Utterly, completely dead—no question

Dogie: A scrubby calf that did not winter well and was anemic from poor nutrition

Douse the lights: Turn the lights out; time to "hit the hay" and go to sleep

Gadabout: Someone who roams or roves about without any apparent business, usually in search of amusement or social activity

Grass widow: A woman who is divorced or separated from her husband

Hear tell: To hear a report of something; to hear of some news or event

Helter-skelter: Haphazard; done in a hurry and without order

Hit the hay: Go to bed

Hold your horses: Stay calm and don't get excited, as in "Hold your horses, we're on our way"

Hornswoggle: To cheat or trick, to pull the wool over one's eyes

Horse feathers: Nonsense, balderdash, obviously ridiculous; foolish or untrue words

Howdy: Informal cowboy greeting; short for "How do you do?"

Let 'er rip: To go faster; to give someone permission to start something

A lick and a promise: A cursory effort, for instance, at painting or tidying up a room or kitchen; also alludes to the perfunctory washing often performed by children, as in "He just gave it a lick and a promise"

Mad as a hornet: Very angry

Maverick: An unbranded animal of unknown ownership; refers to Samuel A. Maverick (1803–70), a Texas rancher and lawyer who took ownership of a bunch of cattle in payment of a bad debt

Make hay while the sun shines: To make the most of the day or an opportunity; to take advantage of your opportunities while they last

Nighthawk: The cattle drive night herder who watches the horses at night to keep them from scattering or being driven off by a rustler

On the dodge: Avoiding consequences by hiding out somewhere or laying low for a while

Persuader: A gun, typically a handgun

Pony up: To pay money that's owed, as in "Pony up that account," or to pony up to the bar to pay for drinks

Ride shank's mare: To use one's legs as a means of transport; to walk or be set afoot without a horse

Ride for the brand: To be loyal and faithful to the ranch and rancher that pays a cowboy's wages; according to Hugh Dempsey's book *The Golden Age of the Canadian*

Cowboy (1995), "Men were known to starve, freeze, fight and die for the outfit that employed them"

Scalawag: A worthless Texas longhorn

Shindig: Usually a fairly small dance or party; a special celebration

Skedaddle: Depart quickly, in haste.

Stampede: The frightened rush of a herd of cattle or horses; in cowboy vernacular, a stampede was "like startin' from the back door of hell on a hot day an' coming' out on the run"

Unmentionables: Underwear or undergarments, which are not discussed in polite society

What in tarnation!: An exclamation used in a surprising or shocking situation; a polite way of saying "What the heck?" or worse; often used by those south of the Mason-Dixon Line

DID YOU  KNOW?

Hornswoggle belongs to a group of what are popularly termed "fancified" words that were particularly popular in the American West in the 19th century. Hornswoggle is one of the earliest of these words, first appearing around 1829. It is likely that these terms were invented to poke fun at the more "sophisticated" folks in the East, who were often perceived as snobs. Other words of this ilk include "absquatulate," which also first appeared in the 1820s; "skedaddle," first used in 1861 in Missouri; and "discombobulate," first recorded in 1916.

What's the Beef?

If not reserved for breeding purposes, cattle of the male sex are "yearlings" for a year, then "steers" until fully grown, and then "beef." On the other hand, a female after her first year

Cattle grazing on native range

becomes a "heifer," then a "two-year-old cow" and so on, until she also goes into the "beef" category, usually once she stops having calves.

Cowboy Slang

Cowboy slang is quite common in contemporary street talk, and most folks probably just take it for granted nowadays. Some of the more common cowboy slang that is popular in both Canada and the United States might include the following:

- "Howdy, pardner!"
- "Cowboy up."
- "Reach for the sky!"
- "Get along, little doggies (or dogies)."
- "Mount up!"
- "Howdy, ma'am."

- "Whoa!"
- "Giddy-up!"
- "Be outta town by high noon!"
- "Y'all come on down now, ya hear."

If you're interested in more cowboy slang, there's a book called *Cowboy Slang: Colorful Cowboy Sayings* (1986) by Edgar R. "Frosty" Potter. This book has an excellent compilation of cowboy slang, with such unique sayings as "He's as slow actin' as wet gunpowder" and "Hot words lead to cold slabs."

In Other Words

Cowboys had unusual words for common objects and situations:

Beans: Pecos strawberries, whistle berries

Beef: slow elk

Biscuits: hot rocks, soda sinkers, shotgun waddin'

Coffee: brown gargle

Complaining: bellyaching

Damn!: Dang!

Dead: belly-up

Fancy, stuck up, snooty: highfalutin'

G** damn it: Dad-blame it

Gravy: Texas butter

Molasses: lick, larrup

Onions: skunk eggs

Pancakes: splatter dabs, wheelers

Stand up at the bar and drink: belly up to the bar

Take a liking to: cotton to

Cowboy Sayings

Cowboys have a unique sense of humor, a way of poking fun at themselves that belies their warm hearts. There are lots of funny cowboy sayings; here are just a few:

- "Always drink upstream from the herd."

- "It's better to keep your mouth shut and look stupid than open it and prove it."

- "Lettin' the cat outta the bag is a whole lot easier than puttin' it back."

- "There are two theories to arguin' with a woman. Neither one works."

FULLY EQUIPPED

A cowboy's saddle was his most prized possession.

Saddle Up!

A western or "cowboy" saddle with a saddle horn was *the* key tool of the trade among cowboys. There are many varieties of western saddles, which differ greatly from English equestrian saddles. A cowboy's saddle was his personal treasure and one of his most prized possessions. There have been many types of saddles used by cowboys over the years, and rodeos have been the drivers behind changes in saddle fashions in terms of their forms and shapes.

DID YOU  KNOW?

His saddle was the last thing a cowboy would part with, and when the saying "He's sold his saddle" was used, it meant that the cowboy was completely broke. The phrase "He's sacked his saddle," meant that the cowboy had died.

Ropes and Lassos

A cowboy had to be skilled in using a rope to lasso cattle.

Part and parcel with a cowboy's saddle would be a horse blanket, bit and reins, a rope (called a lariat in the East) and saddlebags. A rope was essential equipment for a cowboy and was his second most important tool after his saddle, ready to use for a multitude of purposes. The rope would be in the form of a lasso (i.e., a loop of rope designed to be thrown around a target and tightened when pulled) and would be suspended in a neat coil on the right side of his saddle horn.

Breast Collar

A breast collar is common on trail horses and roping horses, and stylized, decorated versions are often seen at horse shows. It is a piece of equipment that runs from the saddle around the chest of the horse, lending both lateral stability and preventing the saddle from sliding back.

Back Cinch

A back cinch (i.e., a second cinch) is often seen on working western saddles, particularly fully rigged roping saddles. Back cinches are made of several thicknesses of leather and are adjusted to be just tight enough to touch the underside of the horse, but not tight enough to provoke discomfort or bucking. The back cinch prevents the rear end of the saddle from rising up in working situations and when roping. It also keeps the saddle fork from digging forward into the horse's withers when a cow is dallied (i.e., tied by wrapping the rope around the saddle horn).

Quirt

Back in the day, cowboys would use a quirt—a flexible, woven leather whip—to control their mounts, especially to strike down a rearing horse that threatened to fall over backward.

Rifles

In the early days, a cowboy would likely be slinging a Winchester repeating rifle in the scabbard hung from his saddle horn. After the Civil War, he would have added a .44-caliber Colt revolver on his hip. Before this war,

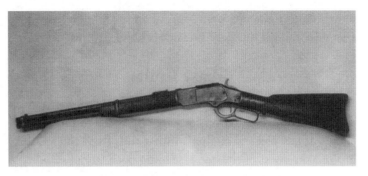

Jesse James' Winchester rifle, circa 1921

cowboys typically used a revolver called the Texas Ranger, which was also made by Colt and brought out in 1842.

The venerable Winchester Model 1873 carbine goes down as one of the most famous of all Winchester rifles. After the Civil War, back in the heyday of cowboys, the Winchester Repeating Arms Company had a veritable monopoly on the firearms business. The Model 1873 was originally chambered for the .44-40 cartridge and was later recalibrated for .38-40 and .32-20 cartridges, which were popular handgun ammunition at the time. It was very practical to carry one type of cartridge that could be chambered interchangeably in both rifles and handguns.

DID YOU  KNOW?

Winchester repeating rifles (i.e., single-barreled rifles that could fire multiple rounds of ammunition) were very popular firearms and among the earliest of their kind. The repeating rifle was known colloquially as "the gun that won the West," and rightly so in its day. These firearms were lever-action rifles manufactured by the Winchester Repeating Arms Company, which also manufactured other rifles with different actions.

WORK WEAR

Cowboy attire grew out of the special needs created by working with cattle, ranch chores and riding a horse, sometimes for extended periods of time, especially during cattle drives. Cowboy apparel has stood the test of time because it has remained relevant throughout history and will remain so as long as the cowboy himself exists, being strong of character, poised, confident and independent.

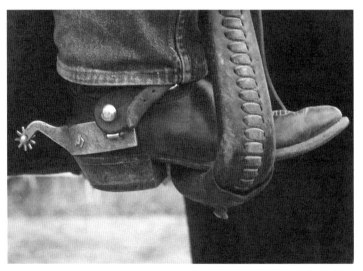

The toe of a cowboy boot is tapered to slide easily into a stirrup.

Cowboy Boots

Cowboy boots are made from leather and have high tops that protect a cowboy's ankles, tapered toes to help guide the boot into the stirrup and high heels to keep the boot from slipping through the stirrup. Although typically made from cowhide, cowboy boots can also be made from more exotic leathers such as snake, ostrich or alligator.

Various places lay claim to having the world's largest cowboy boot, but the record probably goes to Edmonton, Alberta, which boasts a sculptured boot a couple of stories high.

Spurs

Spurs are worn attached to cowboy boots and are used to encourage a horse to go in a particular direction. The metal spurs are attached to the heel of a boot with leather straps. Western spurs usually feature a rotating wheel called a "rowel."

Denim Duds

Blue jeans and jean jackets made of durable denim are standard cowboy attire and have been for a long time. Blue jeans were invented by Jacob Davis and Levi Strauss in 1873 and have been a fashionable urban fad for many years. Jeans wear well and are very sturdy—the main reason they've been a staple of cowboy attire since their invention. Novice horse riders are encouraged to wear "stretch" blue jeans made of polyester fabrics that have some give in them so the riders' legs don't chafe.

Wearing jeans became a symbol of the youth (anti-establishment) counterculture movement during the 1950s after famous Hollywood idol James Dean popular-ized blue jeans in the movie *Rebel Without a Cause* (1955).

A cowboy wouldn't be caught dead without a hat.

Cowboy Hat

Cowboy hats are the signature attire that defines cowboys. All cowboy hats feature a high crown and have a wide brim to protect the eyes and face against the sun, overhanging brush and the elements. There are many styles of cowboy hats—some are made of felt, others of straw and some from leather. The first cowboy hats were made in 1865 by J.B. Stetson.

DID YOU  KNOW?

The first cowboy hat made in 1865 was the open-crowned "Boss of the Plains," and after that came the front-creased

"Carlsbad," destined to become *the* cowboy style. The high-crowned, wide-brimmed, soft-felt western hats that followed remain intimately associated with the cowboy image.

Cowboy Shirt

A cowboy or western shirt is a traditional item of western wear and features a dress yoke (the section of the shirt that joins the collar and the body of the garment in both front and back), a hallmark of cowboy fashion. Usually cowboy shirts are made of denim; however, for dress purposes, the fabric could be plaid. Typically, these shirts have long sleeves to protect a cowboy's forearms from the elements.

DID YOU  KNOW?

Fancy cowboy shirts were popularized in the 1950s by famous western movie stars such as Roy Rogers and Clayton Moore (the Lone Ranger). These shirts were often elaborately decorated with piping, embroidery and contrasting yokes, and featured striking colors.

Bandana

Many working cowboys still wear a loosely tied bandana around their necks to absorb sweat and keep the dust out of their faces when herding cattle.

Chaps and Gloves

Leather gloves and protective chaps are basic tools of the trade for any working cowboy. Chaps are flared, sturdy, leather leggings worn over blue jeans. Unlike trousers, they have no seat and are not joined at the crotch. They're used

Leather chaps shield a cowboy's legs against brush and the elements.

as protection against the elements and to protect a cowboy's legs when riding through brush and working with cattle.

Leather gloves protect a cowboy's hands when riding, working cattle, doing ranch chores and mending barbed-wire fences.

Slicker

A "slicker," or oilskin raincoat, is essential because cowboys work outdoors regardless of the weather. The slicker is typically rolled up neatly behind the cantle of a cowboy's saddle and secured with leather straps.

CANADIAN OUTLAWS

Books About Bad Guys

There are several books that trace the history of outlaws in the Canadian West, but most of these outlaws would not fit with the nature of this book about cowboys. Generally, outlaws were hardened criminals and First Nations individuals who broke the law.

Outlaws & Lawmen of Western Canada, Volume 2 (1983), compiled by Heritage House, details stories about "dramatic crimes in western Canada, including the stories of Jess Williams, who, in 1884, was the first man hanged in Calgary; Almighty Voice, whose murder of a policeman in 1895 caused six other deaths; and BC's Henry Wagner, hanged so quickly that he set a world record."

The billing for *Outlaws of the Canadian West* (2006) written by M.A. Macpherson and published by Lone Pine Publishing states: "The Canadian West has a history littered with tales of robbers and murderers. The frontier days were long before modern forensics and high-tech communications, and the bad guys could hide in plenty of open country before they met up with the mighty Mounties."

Hugh Dempsey's book *The Golden Age of the Canadian Cowboy* (1995) describes a number of notorious horse thieves and cattle rustlers on the Canadian prairies during the 1880s. In the United States, the customary penalty for horse thieving was an unceremonious death by hanging at the hands of local ranchers. Canadian ranchers did not resort to lynching, but there was at least one instance in which the Americans obliged on their behalf in Montana after the thieves crossed the Medicine Line with a herd but without any proof of sale.

Law-abiding Canadians

Unlike the United States, the Canadian West had law and order before it had settlers, and when the North-West Mounted Police arrived in 1874, the land was still the virgin territory of the First Nations and plains bison. By the time the first American cowboys arrived in Canada, the rule of the law was well established, and cowmen accepted this fact as easily as they adapted to the lawless American western frontier. There are apparently only three cases of traditional gunfights reported in Canadian cowboy country, two of which happened in 1885 and the third just after the turn of the 20th century. Warren M. Elofson's book, *Cowboys, Gentlemen and Cattle Thieves* (2000), paints a somewhat different picture of life on the prairies around the turn of the last century, however, where drinking, gambling and prostitution, as well as thefts and assaults, were relatively common. Prostitution flourished in virtually all the towns and was seldom enforced after many years of indifference.

Fort Whoop-Up Outlaws (1869–74)

Fort Whoop-Up was the nickname (later adopted as the official name) of a whiskey-trading post originally called Fort Hamilton, near present-day Lethbridge, Alberta. It was manned by American outlaws who have been described by M.A. Macpherson, author of the book *Outlaws of the Canadian West* (2006), as "a new kind of bandit, intent on trading in illegal booze, [who] packed up and headed north on what was dubbed the Whoop-Up Trail." The Whoop-Up Trail led from Fort Benton, Montana, along the Missouri River

Fort Whoop-up National Historic Site

for 201 miles (324 kilometers) to Fort Whoop-Up at the junction of the St. Mary and Oldman rivers near Lethbridge.

The original fort was built in 1869 by Montana traders John Healy and Al Hamilton to serve as a trading post. Angry Natives burned the fort to the ground in 1870, but it was replaced by an impenetrable new structure in 1874 and later named Fort Whoop-Up.

The Canadian prairies were overrun by unemployed American soldiers after the Civil War ended in 1865, and mercenaries, outlaws and drifters headed north into what was then lawless country. These American whiskey-trading outlaws had no respect for Canada's First Nations people and brought them nothing but misery, disease and suffering by plying them with liquor and guns. The Natives would trade their furs for a tin cup of "rotgut," which was made of raw alcohol, sometimes mixed with tobacco juice for color or with laudanum, an opium substance, along with Jamaican ginger or pepper for throat-burning impact. Fort Whoop-Up also traded in repeating rifles and ammunition.

The American whiskey trade at Fort Whoop-Up and the 1873 Cypress Hills massacre of 30 Assiniboine braves in Saskatchewan by American "wolfers" ultimately led to the creation of the North-West Mounted Police by Canada's first prime minister, Sir John A. Macdonald, in 1873. This force marched west in 1874 and brought law and order to what was then known as the Northwest Territories.

DID YOU  KNOW?

One type of alcohol sold by the Fort Whoop-Up bandits was known as Whoop-Up Bug Juice, a prized concoction spiked with ginger, molasses and red pepper. It was mixed with black chewing tobacco for color, watered down, and then boiled to make "firewater." During the first six months of business at Fort Whoop-Up, the whiskey trade yielded a return of some $50,000 in profits for Healy and Hamilton.

 COWBOY WISDOM
"The man who wears his holster tied down don't do much talkin' with his mouth."

Billy Miner (1843?–1913)

By most accounts, Billy Miner, also known as the "Gray Fox," was Canada's first serial train robber, and his exploits earned him folklore status as the "Gentleman Train Robber." He was the first man to rob the Canadian Pacific Railway, and many of the farmers and ranchers in western Canada didn't see that as a bad thing. At Miner's British Columbia trial, a person responded to a Vancouver reporter's question about public sympathy for Miner with the comment: "Oh, Bill Miner's not so bad. He only robs the CPR once every two years, but the CPR robs us all every day."

Miner was actually an American, born in Bowling Green, Kentucky, around 1843. He ran away from home to become a cowboy, riding as a messenger during the war between the Apaches and the U.S. Army and delivering mail to points east of California. He later started robbing stagecoaches in California, was quickly captured by U.S. marshals and spent four years in San Quentin prison. He didn't learn anything from his time in jail and went back to robbing stagecoaches. He was eventually caught and sentenced to 12 years for a robbery in San Andreas, among others. After serving nine years in prison, Miner traveled to Colorado, Michigan and Arizona, continuing to hold up stagecoaches before being caught once more by U.S. marshals and thrown back in jail at San Quentin in 1881, where he remained until 1901.

By this time, trains had taken over from stagecoaches for delivering gold and cash. Miner drifted north into Oregon and Washington, where he started robbing trains, before eventually crossing the border into Canada in 1904. He settled as a gentleman rancher in the Nicola Valley, near Kamloops, and adopted the alias George Edwards. It wasn't long before he met up with a couple of outlaws, one from Montana and the other from Ontario. Together, they made plans to rob a train heading down the Fraser Canyon with gold dust from the Cariboo Gold Mine in Ashcroft, British Columbia, on September 10, 1904. They carried out a second train robbery on May 8, 1906, east of Kamloops. Authorities offered a cash reward of $15,000 for Miner, dead or alive, and he and his partners were soon arrested near Douglas Lake. After serving time in a New Westminster prison, Miner escaped on August 8, 1907, and skedaddled back to the United States; he was never recaptured in Canada. He took up robbing trains again in the States, was eventually captured and died in Milledgeville State Prison in Georgia on September 2, 1913, at 71 years of age.

DID YOU KNOW?

Billy Miner was best known for his unusual politeness while committing robberies; he was nicknamed the "Gentleman Robber" or the "Gentleman Bandit" and is reputed to have originated the phrase "Hands up!"

Sam Kelly (1859–1937)

Charles "Red" Nelson, alias Sam Kelly, was thought to be the leader of the Nelson-Jones Gang, a group of bank robbers, train robbers and horse and cattle thieves. A Canadian of Irish descent, Kelly was one of the most dangerous and most wanted outlaws of Saskatchewan's Big Muddy Badlands. These badlands are a geographically unique and scenic area in southern Saskatchewan and are probably best known for their caves, which were used by outlaws like Kelly to hide from the U.S. Calvary and other lawmen.

Kelly started life as Charles Nelson. He was born in Nova Scotia and went to Montana to seek his fortune. One of his earliest documented escapades occurred in 1895, when he and an accomplice broke two men out of a jail in Glasgow, Montana. He was also wanted by authorities as a horse thief and a murder suspect. However, when he turned himself in to a sheriff in Plentywood, Montana, in 1904, there wasn't enough evidence to convict him of a single crime.

Kelly returned to the Canadian side of the Big Muddy in 1904. Tired of outlaw life, he became a rancher near Debden, Saskatchewan. He fell ill in 1937 and was taken to a hospital in Battleford, where he died at age 78. Kelly is best known as a leader with Frank Jones of the infamous

Nelson-Jones Gang, one of the main reasons the North-West Mounted Police established a post in the Big Muddy Valley.

AWESOME

Neighbors told stories of Sam Kelly's ability to dehorn a steer with his .30-30 rifle at 100 yards (91 meters), no small feat of marksmanship, particularly with an open sight.

DID YOU  KNOW?

Sam Kelly was described as being about 6 feet tall, slim, 180 pounds, red-haired and red-whiskered with sharp eyes said to be "as cold as a fish." His flaming red hair and beard made him stand out. Kelly was considered the last of Butch Cassidy's Wild Bunch of western outlaws.

AMERICAN OUTLAWS

Jesse James, circa 1882

Jesse Woodson James (1847–82) and Alexander Franklin "Frank" James (1843–1915)

Jesse James and his older brother Frank joined William Clarke Quantrill's Confederate guerillas, known as Quantrill's Raiders, in 1862. The Raiders were regarded as one of the bloodiest fighting forces during the American Civil War. Later, Jesse and

Frank became part of the notorious James-Younger Gang of outlaws that operated out of the state of Missouri. Although the membership of this gang was anchored by the James brothers (Jesse and Frank) and the Younger brothers (Cole, Jim, John and Bob), its membership varied from one robbery to another. During their period of activity, the gang's members robbed banks, trains and stagecoaches in Missouri, Kentucky, Iowa, Texas, Arkansas, Kansas and West Virginia, and managed to elude the law for 17 years.

The James brothers are the most infamous of all the American outlaws, likely because of the publicity associated with their crimes. They had the unsubstantiated reputation of being Robin Hoods of sorts, robbing from the rich and giving to the poor, because they usually robbed federal institutions. After being whipped by Union soldiers on the family farm in Missouri, Jesse no doubt was bitter following the war. The situation was made worse by the federal sanctions against former members of Quantrill's Raiders. Federal law prohibited Quantrill veterans from holding public office, so they could not vote or borrow money from a bank or even belong to a church, which became a civil rights issue with the James brothers. Furthermore, Union soldiers hanged Jesse's father, and though his father survived the hanging, he was brain damaged forever afterward. To make matters even worse, while planning to surrender as the war drew to a close, Jesse was fired upon by Union soldiers at a garrison in Lexington, Missouri, under a white flag and was badly wounded.

On April 3, 1882, Jesse James was shot in the back of the head and killed by Robert "Bob" Ford, a member of the gang who was living in the James' house and who hoped to collect the $10,000 reward on Jesse's head. After Jesse was killed, his brother Frank was arrested after he surrendered to the governor of Missouri. Frank was eventually aquitted at trials in Missouri and Alabama.

The Man Who Shot Jesse James

Robert Ford was widely scorned after his cowardly shooting of Jesse James. On the morning of June 8, 1892, Ed O'Kelley entered Ford's tent saloon in Creede, Colorado, pulled a double-barreled, sawed-off shotgun from his coat and fired both barrels into either Ford's back, head or upper body (there is conflicting information regarding just where he was shot).

Ford was first interred in Creede, Colorado, but was later reburied at the Richmond Cemetery in Richmond, Missouri, with "The man who shot Jesse James" inscribed on his grave marker. Edward O'Kelley was jailed for eight years for his act according to some sources, while others claim he was convicted and given a 20-year sentence in a Colorado penitentiary. However, after serving 10 years, O'Kelley was released in 1902. Two years later, in January 1904, lawmen gunned O'Kelley down in the streets of Oklahoma City.

AWESOME

A pistol belonging to Jesse James was tipped to sell for over $1.6 million at an auction in 2013, 130 years after his death. The Colt .45 revolver was a favorite of the notorious gunslinger. Experts have described James' gun as one of the most significant items ever to appear at auction.

DID YOU  KNOW?

There have been 15 movies featuring Jesse James, the most recent being *The Assassination of Jesse James by the Coward Robert Ford* (2007), written and directed by Andrew Dominik and starring Brad Pitt.

Belle Starr (1848–89)

Myra Maebelle Shirley Reed Starr, better known as Belle Starr, was a rather notorious American outlaw, though she has been popularized as a legendary western heroine. She was born on a farm near Carthage, Missouri, and was known as Mae to her family. During the Civil War, after a Union attack on Carthage in 1864, the Shirleys moved to Scyene, Texas. According to legend, it was at Scyene that the Shirley family became associated with a number of Missouri-born criminals, including Jesse and Frank James and the Younger brothers. Mae Shirley reputedly knew them all because she had grown up with them in Missouri.

In 1866, Mae was apparently coerced into marrying James C. "Jim" Reed in a horseback ceremony, and he turned to a life of crime after their marriage. Reed was killed in Paris, Texas, in 1874 by John Morris, a man he thought was a trusted companion. Morris shot Reed for a large reward, which he never collected because Mae would not positively identify Reed's body. She then went on to marry Bruce Younger on May 15, 1880, but the marriage only lasted a few weeks, and in 1880, Belle married a Cherokee man named Sam Starr and settled with the Starr family in the Indian Territory of Oklahoma. It was then that she became known as Belle Starr and allegedly became adept at organizing, planning and fencing for rustlers, horse thieves and bootleggers. She also harbored them from the law.

Belle became known as the "Bandit Queen" for supporting her Cherokee outlaw friends. She reportedly gave birth to a couple of illegitimate children and may have engaged in prostitution on occasion. In 1883, she was charged with horse theft and served nine months in prison, and later escaped conviction of a charge of theft in 1886.

On Christmas Eve in 1886, Sam Starr was involved in a gun-fight with Officer Frank West in which both Starr and West were killed. Belle's life as an outlaw ended with her husband's death, but by this time, accounts of her outlaw adventures had been embellished in dime novels, and she was considered a celebrity of sorts. She remarried a younger Cherokee man named Jim July, but because of her dime-novel status refused to take July's surname. On Sunday, February 3, 1889, Belle was shot in the back of the head during an ambush, then shot again in the chest and neck. She was 41 when she died. The identity of her assassin remains unknown, though there were several suspects.

Belle Starr has gone down in history as a horse thief, cattle rustler, suspected robber of stagecoaches, perennial concubine and protector of desperate criminals.

DID YOU KNOW?

Belle Star was reportedly a crack shot. She rode sidesaddle while dressed in a black velvet riding habit and a plumed hat, carrying two pearl-handled pistols and with cartridge belts fastened across her hips. The caption beneath a studio portrait of Belle Starr reads "Queen of the Oklahoma Outlaws."

The Dalton Gang

The Dalton Gang was a group of American outlaws from Indian Territory (now the state of Oklahoma) and gained notoriety from 1890 to 1892. These outlaws were also known as the Dalton Brothers Gang because three of its members were brothers, though not all the gang members came from the Dalton family, and not all the Dalton brothers were in the gang. The gang specialized in bank and train robberies mainly in California and Oklahoma.

There were 13 children in the Dalton family. The three Dalton brothers involved in the gang were Gratton "Grat" (born 1861), Bob (born 1869) and Emmett (born 1871). Bob was the leader of the gang. Some of the Daltons were lawmen. Frank (born 1859) was a respected deputy marshal, and both Bob and Grat served as lawmen before turning to a life of crime. They were sometimes accompanied by Emmett when they stole horses and committed other minor crimes.

The Dalton family was related to the Younger family through their mother, Adeline, who was a member of the James-Younger Gang. Some of the Dalton boys admired the Younger brothers because of their dime-novel status. The Dalton Gang gained notoriety as folk heros not only for their daring robberies, but also because the settlers disliked both banks and railroads for various reasons. During a bold double bank robbery (the C.M. Condon and Company Bank and the First National Bank across the street) by the Dalton Gang in Coffeyville, Kansas, on October 5, 1892, Grat and Bob were both killed during a shootout with local citizens and lawmen, and Emmett was badly wounded.

DID YOU KNOW?

Amazingly, Emmett Dalton was shot many times during the Coffeyville shootout (some reports claim 23 times, other reports mention 27 times) before falling from his horse and being subdued by local citizens. Despite his wounds, he miraculously survived, was tried and given a life sentence, which he served in Kansas State Prison. He was pardoned in 1907 for good behavior, moved to California and became real estate agent, author and actor. He died in 1937 at age 66.

John Wesley Hardin (1853–95)

John Wesley Hardin was an American outlaw, gunfighter and charismatic folk hero of the Old West and is sometimes referred to as the "Texas Jesse James." He developed a reputation as a notorious gunfighter, credited to his lightning speed with a handgun. He had killed more than 21 men by the time he was 24 and perhaps as many as 40 during his lifetime. The first person he killed was a bully who came after him with a club when he was only 15 years old (some reports say he was only 12 at the time). Although he claimed that he killed many of his victims in self-defense, he nonetheless became a highly wanted man in the Southwest.

In 1877, Hardin was taken prisoner and tried for the murder of Sheriff Charlie Webb. Despite swearing to a jury that he had killed Webb in self-defense, Hardin was found guilty of second-degree murder and so was spared being hanged. Instead, he was sentenced to 21 years hard labor at the Rusk Prison in Huntsville, Texas. Hardin served 16 years of his term and went on to become a lawyer, having studied law while incarcerated. He was considered a good citizen and a community leader in El Paso, Texas, before his death. Hardin was killed with a bullet to the back of his head by an El Paso lawman named John Selman in the Acme Saloon on the night of August 19, 1895. Convinced that Selman acted in self-defense, a jury acquitted the lawman of murdering Hardin. Hardin's last words were "Four sixes to beat."

DID YOU  KNOW?

Hardin's favorite weapons were a pair of matched Colt .45 revolvers, which he kept in special chest pockets sewn into his vest or tucked into his waistband between his shirt and undershirt.

Billy the Kid (1859–81)

Billy the Kid, born Henry McCarty in New York City, alias William "Billy" H. Bonney and Henry Antrim, was a 19th-century American gunman. He developed a reputation for being able to escape from almost any jail, and legend has it that he killed 21 men before his 21st birthday. The first man that Billy killed was a blacksmith named Cahill. A justice of the peace ruled the incident as being criminal, and Billy was declared guilty and jailed, but managed to escape.

Billy the Kid participated in the Lincoln County War in New Mexico, a conflict between established town merchants Lawrence Murphy and James Dolan and competing business interests headed by cattleman John Tunstall and lawyer Alexander McSween. Following a long-running feud with another Lincoln County cattle gang, Billy the Kid's gang was ambushed by Sheriff Pat Garrett on December 19, 1880. The Kid was captured two days before Christmas and was sentenced to death for the murder of a Sheriff Brady on March 31, 1878.

Billy escaped jail by killing two of his captors two weeks before he was to be hanged and made national headlines in the U.S. Billy had been on the run for three months when Sheriff Pat Garrett tracked him down on the Maxwell ranch near Fort Sumner, New Mexico. Garrett fired two shots at the Kid in a darkened room, killing the outlaw instantly with a shot above his heart (the second shot apparently missed). A coroner's jury acquitted Garrett of allegations that he had unjustifiably shot Billy, declaring it justifiable homicide.

Billy the Kid, circa 1880

DID YOU  KNOW?

One of the few remaining artifacts of Billy the Kid's life is a 2×3-inch (5×7-centimeter) ferrotype (an early type of photograph) taken by an unknown photographer sometime in late 1879 or early 1880. It is apparently the only known image authentic of the outlaw. The ferrotype sold at auction on June 25, 2011, for $2.3 million.

Robert LeRoy Parker, also known as Butch Cassidy, 1893

Butch Cassidy (1866–1908)

Robert LeRoy Parker is best known as Butch Cassidy, one of the most notorious of all outlaws in the United States. He adopted the alias Cassidy, one of many he used, in honor of a man named Mike Cassidy, who tutored him in cattle rustling and horse thievery. He used George as a first name until he was nicknamed "Butch," having worked for a time as a cattle butcher. One of his childhood nicknames was

"Sallie," which he detested. Although a Mormon, Cassidy was a notorious horse thief, rustler, train and bank robber and the leader of the Wild Bunch, also known as the Hole-in-the-Wall Gang.

After several years of a life in crime in the U.S., the pressures of being pursued, notably by the Pinkerton Detective Agency, forced Butch Cassidy to flee the country with an accomplice, Harry Alonzo Longabaugh, known as the Sundance Kid, and Longabaugh's girlfriend, Etta Place. The Pinkerton Agency was relentless in tracking the whereabouts of Butch and Sundance, and the trio first fled to Argentina and then to Bolivia. There's also speculation that they may have spent some time in Chile. Canada was not an option because there was too much law and order thanks to the Mounties, who had already developed a reputation for always getting their man.

Although Butch and Sundance did some ranching after they arrived in Argentina, it wasn't long before they resumed robbing banks. The two outlaws were thought to have been killed by soldiers in a shootout in San Vicente, Bolivia, in November 1908. Although this shooting has been long disputed, authorities believe that Butch Cassidy put a bullet through the Sundance Kid's head, then killed himself. The two bodies were buried nearby. Over the years, skeptics who believed that Butch and Sundance did not die in Bolivia claim that the Bolivian authorities never positively identified the two men who were killed in San Vicente. However, aliases linked to the outlaws were indirectly linked to the shootout.

There is apparently no evidence that conclusively identifies the two men killed in San Vicente, so the truth about the death of Butch and Sundance has never been fully settled. Some historical evidence suggests that Butch Cassidy faked his death and returned to the United States with a new name:

Harry Alonzo Longabaugh, also known as the Sundance Kid, and Etta Place, circa 1880

William T. Phillips. Back in his home country, it's alleged that he lived another three decades, making a living as a machinist before passing away from cancer in Spokane, Washington, in 1937.

DID YOU  KNOW?

The Wild Bunch's last express car train robbery (of the *Coast Flyer*) took place on the Great Northern Railroad near Wagner, Montana, on July 3, 1901. At the time, some American railroad companies were offering rewards for train robbers, dead or alive, though the Great Northern Railroad did not follow this practice.

DID YOU  KNOW?

In 1991, a scientific team excavated the graves of the two criminals killed in the shootout in San Vicente, Bolivia, which were believed to have been Butch Cassidy and the Sundance Kid. However, DNA samples did not match those of any relatives of the outlaws. Some people claim that means the two men killed in the famous shootout were not the legendary duo, whereas others say the graves were simply not those of Butch and Sundance but of two other people buried in the town at a different time altogether.

RIDING AND ROPING

Saddle bronc riding

The History of Rodeos

Rodeos are the ultimate showcase of a cowboy's riding skills. These events date back to antiquity and are the present-day embodiment of cowboys to many people. The early rodeos of the 1820s and 1830s in the western United States and northern Mexico were informal events, with cowboys and vaqueros testing their working skills against one another. Although most riders traditionally rode for a predetermined length of time, the puncher on the ranch had to ride until the horse was broke and subdued.

DID YOU  KNOW?

The town of Prescott, Arizona, claims the distinction of having held the first professional rodeo in 1888, as it charged admission and awarded trophies, contrary to claims that the first American rodeo was held in Cheyenne, Wyoming, in 1872.

Frontier Days celebration, Cheyenne, Wyoming, 1910

Finding a Wider Audience

Between 1890 and 1910, rodeos went public, sometimes combined with Wild West shows featuring stars such as Buffalo Bill Cody and Annie Oakley. By 1910, several major rodeos were well established in western North America, including the Calgary Stampede in Alberta, the Pendleton Round-Up in Oregon and Cheyenne Frontier Days in Wyoming. Literally thousands of rodeos are held worldwide each year in far-off countries such as Australia, Brazil, Mexico and the Philippines, not just in Canada and the U.S.

Rodeo Events

Events that are typical of most rodeos include bareback bronc riding, saddle bronc riding, bull riding, steer wrestling (bulldogging), team roping, tie-down roping and barrel racing.

 COWBOY WISDOM

"The only good reason to ride a bull is to meet a nurse."

DID YOU  KNOW?

The first official rodeo in Canada was held in Raymond, Alberta, in 1902.

Rodeo Terminology

Barrier: A breakaway rope pulled across the roping chutes; contestants cannot cross the barrier until the steer or calf enters the arena

Barrelman: A rodeo performer whose main (and dangerous) job is to distract the bull by providing an alternate target to the rider; also known as a rodeo clown or entertainer

Bronc: A wild, untamed horse used in bucking-horse competitions

Bulldogger: A steer wrestler

Dally: To wrap the end of a lariat around a saddle horn once an animal has been roped

Flank strap: A sheepskin-lined breakaway strap passed around the flank of a bronc or bull; encourages the animal to kick out behind rather than rear up

Rodeo clown

Go-round: One round of competition in a rodeo

Hazer: In steer wrestling, the cowboy who rides along the right-hand side of a steer to try to keep it running in a straight line

Header: In team roping, the cowboy who ropes the steer's head

Heeler: In team roping, the cowboy who ropes the steer's hind feet

Hung up: In bareback riding, saddle bronc and bull riding, when a competitor is unable to free his hand from the rigging or bullrope, he is said to be "hung up"; can be very dangerous to the rider and may cause serious injury

Mark out: To "mark out," a bronc rider's heels must be above the horse's shoulders when the horse's front feet hit the ground on the first jump out of the chute; if the contestant misses the mark out, there's no score

Pickup man: A horseback rider who rescues or "picks up" a bronc rider from his mount after a ride

Prize purse: The total amount of prize money that is distributed among the contestants

Qualified ride: For a ride to be "qualified," that is, for a cowboy to receive a score in a roughstock event, he must remain mounted on a bronc or bull for eight seconds with his free hand not contacting the animal

Rank: An adjective used to describe a roughstock animal that is very difficult to ride

Rigging: The leather pad in bareback riding or the rope in bull riding that a cowboy holds onto to avoid being bucked off

Roughstock events: Bareback bronc, saddle bronc and bull riding events that are scored by judges

Stock contractor: A stock agent who provides rodeo animals

Timed events: Events based on speed (i.e., tie-down roping, steer wrestling, team roping and barrel racing)

Timers: Officials who use clocks to track timed events

Women's Events

Pole bending: A timed event in which a horse and rider must run a serpentine path around six poles arranged in a line.

Breakaway roping: A variation of calf roping in which a calf is roped, but not thrown and tied, by a mounted rider.

Steer undecorating: The female version of steer wrestling in which a cowgirl must catch up to a steer and remove the ribbon attached to its back. As in steer wrestling, the cowgirl is allowed a "hazer" to aid her in lining up the charging steer.

Team roping: Also known as "heading and heeling," this event features a steer and two mounted riders. It is the only event in which women and men compete together. The first roper is referred to as the "header," the person who ropes the front of

Women's barrel racing

the steer (usually around the horns, but it is also legal for the rope to go around the neck or one horn and the nose, resulting in what is called a "half head"), and the second rider is the "heeler," who must rope the steer by its hind feet, with a five-second penalty added to the end time if only one leg is roped.

Rodeo Queen

A rodeo queen is a very talented (and often gorgeous) woman, and in many ways, she is *the* public face of rodeos. She represents her particular rodeo, association or region, usually for a year, and she must excel in public-speaking, horsemanship and general knowledge of rodeos. Rodeo queens spend their time professionally representing their title at various rodeos, parades, public events, television and radio interviews, school events and charity events. It's not unusual for a rodeo queen to make literally hundreds of public appearances annually.

There are three nationwide pageants in the United States: Miss Rodeo America, Miss Rodeo USA and the National High School Rodeo Association Queen Contest. In Canada, there's the Miss Rodeo Canada pageant. In addition, most rodeos in both Canada and the U.S. have their own pageants and rodeo queens.

Animal Welfare

Animal care is often an issue at rodeos and remains a concern and priority of rodeo associations. Rodeo officials consult with veterinarians to ensure that rodeo stock are treated humanely and in adherence to codes of practice related to animal care. The larger events have a full-time team of veterinarians on hand, and a veterinarian checks each animal daily. Some critics feel that rodeos should be banned, particularly if an animal dies during one of the events.

Opponents such as those featured on the SHARK (Showing Animals Respect and Kindness) website (www.sharkonline. org) state categorically: "Forget the myth of rodeos as all-American sport. Modern rodeos are cruel and deadly for animals." This allegation is contrary to the best interests of rodeo officials and participants. No one wants to harm rodeo stock, which are cared for by those who live, love and work with animals every day of their lives. There's actually more danger to the riders than to the rodeo stock.

Unfortunately, it's not possible to clinically treat most large animals or calves used in calf-roping competitions that suffer broken legs (a rare event) even though the cost-benefit equation is near neutral, so economics are not really a factor. Rodeo contestants develop their skills while working on ranches, but there's no doubt that rodeo prizes are the main attraction nowadays. However, rodeo contestants have the mindset that what they're doing is basically an extension of what working cowboys do day in and day out, as a matter of business.

CANADIAN RODEOS

The Calgary Stampede, Calgary

The Calgary Stampede, the Greatest Outdoor Show on Earth

The Calgary Stampede, held annually in Calgary, Alberta, has long been billed as "the Greatest Outdoor Show on Earth." The event originated in 1912, though its roots go back to 1886. Held annually each July, the Stampede features a kickoff parade, one of the world's largest rodeos, a midway, concerts and stage shows, agricultural competitions, chuckwagon racing and exhibitions by First Nations groups. In 2012, the Calgary Stampede set an all-time attendance record of 1,409,371. The event has routinely attracted over one million people annually during the past decade, and attendance has held steady between one million and 1.25 million every year since 1986. Critics comment that there's not much more room for people inside Stampede Park until its next expansion.

According to Stampede officials, the Calgary Stampede Rodeo is the world's richest tournament-style rodeo and featured over $2 million in prize money in 2013. Rodeo contestants are divided into two pools. The top four money winners in each pool advance to Showdown Sunday. The remaining six competitors in each pool compete on Wild Card Saturday, and the top two in each event also advance to Showdown Sunday—rodeo's richest afternoon with over $1 million to be awarded. All the ballyhoo leads up to a one shot, go-for-broke performance with winners taking home the Calgary Stampede Championship and $100,000.

DID YOU  KNOW?

The Alberta Legislature has considered making rodeo the official sport of the province of Alberta.

Canadian Finals Rodeo, Edmonton

The Canadian Finals Rodeo (CFR) takes place every November in Edmonton, Alberta, and is the final event of the Canadian Professional Rodeo Association season. The CFR celebrated its 40th anniversary in 2013. The event offers one of the richest purses in Canadian rodeo, usually worth over $1 million. According to the latest news release, "Each November since 1974, the greatest rodeo athletes and stock in the nation descend on the Northlands grounds and inject the City of Edmonton with a dose of adrenaline unmatched by any other sport."

Championship titles are awarded to individuals who earn the most money in his or her event: bareback riding, steer wrestling (also known as bulldogging), team roping (divided into "headers" and "heelers" in 1995), saddle bronc riding, tie-down roping (formerly calf roping), barrel racing and bull riding. According to Edmonton Tourism, "For fans, this national championship is the Super Bowl of the Canadian rodeo circuit. Celebrating its 40th year in Edmonton, competitors vie for some of Canada's top prizes in rodeo. This year's [2013] purse totals $1.47 million."

DID YOU KNOW?

Roger Lacasse, from Mirabel, Quebec, not only qualified for the Canadian Finals Rodeo, but he also won the bareback riding title twice, in 1998 and 2004. The first and only Quebec cowboy in history to participate in the national championships, Lacasse has been selected for induction into the Canadian Pro Rodeo Hall of fame.

Steer wrestling at the Ponoka Stampede

Ponoka Stampede, Ponoka

The Ponoka Stampede is one of Alberta's biggest rodeos, attracting 65,000 spectators every year. The event celebrated its 77th anniversary in 2013, testament to its long-standing popularity. It is held in late June and over the Canada Day long weekend, just before the Calgary Stampede, and many cowboys regard it as a warm-up for the Greatest Outdoor Show on Earth. This is one of Alberta's top pro rodeos, but it also features many other attractions such as the Kids' Wild Pony Race, which is worth the price of admission itself.

DID YOU KNOW?

A long-standing trick that bull riders and bareback bronc riders still use to keep from being bucked off is to put tar or resin on the hand that's held in the bareback rigging.

Cranbrook Pro Rodeo, Cranbrook

Held annually in Cranbrook, British Columbia, the Cranbrook Pro Rodeo marked its 27th anniversary in 2013. It continues to be a popular stop on the Canadian Professional Rodeo Association roster.

Smithers Fall Fair and Rodeo, Smithers

Part of the annual Bulkley Valley Exhibition (BVX) held in Smithers, BC, in late August, the Smithers Fall Fair and Rodeo is hosted by the BVX and the Smithers Rodeo Club.

Williams Lake Stampede, Williams Lake

In 2014, BC's Williams Lake Stampede will celebrate its 88th anniversary over the Canada Day holiday weekend. This rodeo features Canadian Professional Rodeo Association action in six main events: bull riding, ladies barrel racing, bareback and saddle bronc riding, steer wrestling and tie-down roping.

DID YOU KNOW?

The star goalie of the storied Montreal Canadiens National Hockey League team, Carey Price, has competed on the British

Columbia rodeo circuit. He finished third among 32 entries in the team roping competition at the Smithers Rodeo in 2010.

Wood Mountain Rodeo

The Wood Mountain Rodeo, held in Wood Mountain Regional Park east of Grasslands National Park in southern Saskatchewan, is Canada's oldest continuous rodeo event and will celebrate 125 years in 2014. Located within the regional park are the Rodeo Ranch Museum, Homestead Museum, Sitting Bull Monument, baseball diamonds, campsites, a play area, concessions, a swimming pool and hiking and bicycling trails. This event started back in 1889, pre-dating Canada's first official rodeo, which was held in Raymond, Alberta, in 1902.

Interior Provincial Exhibition and Stampede, Armstrong

The Interior Provincial Exhibition (IPE) and Stampede, held in Armstrong, BC, was rated as one of the top 10 Canadian fairs and exhibitions in a 2011 vacation guide published by *Canadian Cowboy Country* magazine. It's the second largest fair in the province, after the Pacific National Exhibition, which is held in Vancouver.

Armstrong is located in the Okanagan Valley north of Vernon. The event celebrated its 114th year in 2013, a proud accomplishment. The IPE and rodeo is noted as being "one of the few surviving authentic agricultural fairs across Canada, with a long history of local dedication" and is part of the Canadian Professional Rodeo Association's Wrangler Canadian Tour. This popular annual fair and rodeo is held at the end of August and drew about 150,000 visitors in 2013.

Val Marie Indoor Rodeo, Val Marie

The popular Val Marie Indoor Rodeo, held in Val Marie, Saskatchewan, will celebrate its 50th anniversary in September 2014. Sanctioned by the Canadian Cowboys' Association, the event features saddle and bareback bronc riding, bull riding, steer wrestling, ladies' barrel racing, tie-down roping, team roping and junior steer riding.

Canadian Cowboys' Association Finals Rodeo, Regina

The Canadian Cowboys' Association Finals Rodeo has been held every November in Regina at the Canadian Western Agribition since 2005. It attracts more than 20,000 to the Saskatchewan capital.

Over the 2012 season, the CCA sanctioned 60 rodeos across Canada, from Alberta to Ontario, as well as another 13 that were co-sanctioned, and over $1.2 million was paid out in prize money. Each season culminates in the finals rodeo.

Festival Western de Saint-Tite, Quebec

It may sound hard to believe, but the Festival Western de Saint-Tite, held annually in Saint-Tite, Quebec, every September, is billed as the second largest rodeo in Canada. The event has been running since 1967 and now awards over $300,000 in prize money. Voted Best Outdoor Rodeo in North America since 1999, Saint-Tite's festival attracts around 450,000 visitors every year.

AMERICAN RODEOS

Rodeos are held in over two dozen states in the U.S., some even in far-off, unlikely states such as Florida, Maryland, New Jersey and Wisconsin. These events are firmly embedded in all the "western" states and have been for many years. It just isn't feasible to list all the American rodeos here, but some of the more interesting and unique events are covered in this section.

Fiesta de los Vaqueros, Tucson, Arizona

The Fiesta de los Vaqueros is a weeklong rodeo event held in February, which is early spring in Tucson, and marks the beginning of the rodeo season in the United States. The event features what is billed as the world's largest rodeo parade.

White Mountain Apache Tribal Fair and Rodeo, Prescott, Arizona

The event that claims to be the world's oldest rodeo, the White Mountain Apache Tribal Fair and Rodeo, is held annually in late August. It starts on a Wednesday night with the Thunder on the Mountain Bullbash and ends with the rodeo finals on the following Monday. It will celebrate its 89th anniversary in 2014.

Payson Rodeos, Payson, Arizona

Payson hosts a number of rodeos every year, but the biggest is the August Doin's. Considered the world's oldest *continuously held* rodeo, it has been held annually since 1884. (Cheyenne, Wyoming, claims to have held the first rodeo in the U.S. in 1872.) The weeklong event is held on the third weekend in August.

DID YOU KNOW?

The area around Payson is called Zane Grey Country because the celebrated author not only wrote several books about the area, but also owned land near the town.

Steer wrestling

California Rodeo, Salinas, California

The Salinas Rodeo is a major stop on the professional rodeo circuit each July. It is also the largest rodeo in California and one of the top 10 rodeos in the U.S. The event began in 1911 as a Wild West show and had its origins in the days of the Spanish rancheros' annual spring and fall roundups. Rodeo contestants compete for almost $400,000 in prize money and the coveted gold-and-silver Salinas belt buckle. This annual event draws over 50,000 spectators.

Dodge City Roundup Rodeo, Dodge City, Kansas

The Dodge City Roundup Rodeo is the centerpiece of the Dodge City Days Festival, the second largest community event in Kansas. At its inception in 1977, the roundup had 175 contestants with a payout of $8200, which has grown to about 800 contestants and a payout of $254,000 (2013). It is the only Professional Rodeo Cowboys Association Wrangler Million Dollar Tour rodeo in Kansas and is the richest in contestant payout in the state.

National Finals Rodeo, Las Vegas, Nevada

The National Finals Rodeo (NFR), organized by the Professional Rodeo Cowboys Association (PRCA), is the premier championship rodeo event in the U.S. Popularly known as the "Super Bowl of Rodeo," it's an annual 10-day show to determine the champions in seven main events and to crown the World All-Around Rodeo Champion Cowboy, an honor awarded to the highest-earning cowboy who has competed in rodeo events throughout the year.

DID YOU  KNOW?

The PRCA established the National Finals Rodeo in 1958 to determine the world champion in each of rodeo's seven main events: tie-down roping, steer wrestling, bull riding, saddle bronc riding, bareback bronc riding, barrel racing and team roping. However, the world championship steer roping competition has always been held separately from this event.

Pendleton Round-Up, Pendleton, Oregon

The first Pendleton Round-Up rodeo took place on September 29, 1910, and has been an annual event ever since. This popular rodeo is held during the second full week of September and attracts upwards of 50,000 visitors. According to their website, the key to the success of the rodeo is community participation and the involvement of Native Americans and female rodeo performers. Local news-papers have summed up a characterization of this rodeo that has stood the test of time: "In good times and bad, Pendleton has gone on with the Round-Up."

Pendleton is also famous for its Pendleton Blended Canadian Whisky—commonly known as "The Cowboy Whisky"—which is distilled in Canada, imported, bottled and marketed by Hood River Distillers of Hood River, Oregon. A portion of the proceeds from each bottle is donated to the Pendleton Round-Up.

DID YOU  KNOW?

In 1914, Bertha Blanchett, wife of cowboy Del Blanchett, came within 12 points of winning the all-around rodeo title.

RODEO ASSOCIATIONS

Rodeo associations promote and govern rodeos throughout North America and in other parts of the world. The backbone of the sport, they ensure its continuation and bring the excitement of the sport to audiences everywhere.

Chuckwagon racing

Canadian Professional Rodeo Association

The Canadian Professional Rodeo Association (CPRA) is the official sanctioning and governing body of professional rodeos in Canada. Their head office is in Airdrie, Alberta. The CPRA sanctioned 62 rodeos in Canada in 2012, with a combined total payout of over $5.1 million. The organization is committed to maintaining the highest standards, ensuring that every CPRA-sanctioned event is managed with fairness and competence and that the livestock used is healthy and cared for to the highest standards. Approximately 1400 members are represented by the association's board of directors.

DID YOU  KNOW?

CPRA-sanctioned rodeos create a positive economic impact on the cities and towns that host them. For example, the Canadian Finals Rodeo in Edmonton generates more than $50 million annually for the local community. As well, professional rodeos in North America raise in excess of $30 million for local and international charities each year.

Professional Rodeo Cowboys Association

Created in 1936, the Professional Rodeo Cowboys Association (PRCA) is an organization whose members compete in rodeos throughout North America, primarily in the United States. The association sanctions rodeo venues and events throughout the PRCA circuit. Its championship event is the Wrangler National Finals Rodeo, held annually in Las Vegas. The PRCA has its headquarters in Colorado Springs, Colorado.

DID YOU  KNOW?

Eight events and 10 championships are sanctioned by the PRCA: All-Around Cowboy, bareback and saddle bronc riding, steer wrestling, team roping ("headers and heelers"), tie-down roping, barrel racing and bull riding. All-Around Cowboy is an award given to the competitor who is the most successful in two or more events. Trevor Brazile, who hails from Decatur, Texas, has won the PCRA All-Around Cowboy event a remarkable 10 times.

Canadian Cowboys' Association

The Canadian Cowboys Association (CCA) is the largest semi-professional rodeo association in Canada. Currently based out of Regina, Saskatchewan, the CCA was founded in 1963 with 60 members. It has now grown to almost 1000 members across five Canadian provinces. Many CCA contestants have gone on to become professionals and compete in events such as the Canadian and National Finals rodeos. The CCA's mission is to promote the sport of rodeo, and the organization is committed to attracting new cowboys and cowgirls, increasing the number of spectators and attracting the media to the tradition and heritage of rodeos and the families that make up the CCA.

DID YOU KNOW?

The Canadian Cowboys' Association celebrated its 50th anniversary in 2013.

Cowboys Professional Rodeo Association

The Cowboys Professional Rodeo Association (CPRA) represents professional cowboys in the United States. Their head office is in Dayton, Texas. Established in 1992 by a group of producers and rodeo contestants, the CPRA held its first finals rodeo in Lufkin, Texas, and contributed $25,000 in prize money. As of 2011, their membership was at an all-time high of 1110 members.

DID YOU KNOW?

In 2011, the Cowboys Professional Rodeo Association celebrated its 19th annual finals, and total payouts amounted to $1,766,349.

Woman cutting out a calf at a rodeo

Women's Professional Rodeo Association

The Women's Professional Rodeo Association (WPRA) claims to be the oldest women's sports organization in the U.S. The association was established in 1948 by a group of Texas ranch women who apparently wanted to add a little color and femininity to the sport of rodeo. Considered quite a major move at the time, 38 women met in a hotel in San Angelo, Texas, on February 28, 1948, to change the way they were being treated in the male-dominated world of rodeos. These women banded together to found the very first professional sports association created solely for women by women—the Girls Rodeo Association.

British Columbia Rodeo Association

The British Columbia Rodeo Association was established in 1988 and became the primary governing body for rodeos in BC when the Interior Rodeo Association, Yellowhead Cowboys Association and Vancouver Island Rodeo Association were amalgamated. This merger created a strong organization, combining decades of rodeo experience from all corners of the province. Over 500 members compete annually at rodeos throughout British Columbia.

British Columbia Little Britches Rodeo Association

The BC Little Britches Rodeo Association is where young cowboys and cowgirls get their start in the sport of rodeo. A non-profit organization, the BC Little Britches Rodeo Association, along with local rodeo clubs throughout the province, hosts rodeos in spring, summer and fall. Various communities from Chilliwack in the Fraser Valley to Oliver and Vernon in the Okanagan Valley to several Interior towns, including 100 Mile House and as far north as Prince George, participate in this association.

Canadian Girls Rodeo Association

The Canadian Girls Rodeo Association (CGRA) has its headquarters in Calgary, Alberta, and represents Canadian girls' rodeo interests. Events covered by the CGRA include cow riding, junior and open barrel racing, junior pole bending, ladies pole bending, junior breakaway, tie-down roping, steer undecorating, goat tying, junior goat tying, team roping (header) and team roping (heeler).

Arkansas Cowboys Association

The Arkansas Cowboys Association (ACA) consists of cowboys, cowgirls and rodeo stock contractors throughout Arkansas. The association was formed in 1976 by a small group of rodeo contestants and stock contractors. Nowadays, under a governing board of directors, the ACA is one of the largest rodeo associations in the state. Competitors vie for large prize money and points to make the ACA Finals each year in October.

Justa Cowboy Association

According to their website, the Justa Cowboy Association "is an Afro-American organization that promotes the sport of rodeo with the highest professional conduct and sportsmanship." The association works to preserve the cowboy way of life and honor the contributions of African American cowboys to the sport of rodeo. They sponsor a number of "Black rodeos" annually, with an emphasis on providing family entertainment. Additionally, the organization carries on the cowboy tradition of "passing the hat" to fund scholarships for local students.

Cowboy Mounted Shooting Association

The Cowboy Mounted Shooting Association (CMSA) bills itself as "the Fastest Growing Equestrian Sport in the Nation." According to their website (www.cmsaevents.com), "mounted contestants compete in this fast-action, timed event using two .45-caliber, single-action revolvers, each loaded with five rounds of specially prepared blank ammunition." Western dress is required for competitors, and riders shoot at balloons. Scores are based on time and accuracy, with penalties assessed for missing balloons, not running the course correctly, dropping a gun and falling off the horse. The CMSA has a variety of levels of competition for everyone, ranging from novices to seasoned professionals.

The Extreme Cowboy Association

Established in 2008 and based in Bluff Dale, Texas, the Extreme Cowboy Association (EXCA) bills itself as the original and only recognized association for the sport of extreme cowboy racing. The Extreme Cowboy Race was established by Craig Cameron, the "Original Extreme Cowboy." According to online sources, "The sport has been featured at the Calgary Stampede, as the 'Cowboy Up Challenge,' and at Canada's

Outdoor Equine Expo [in Burlington, Ontario], while experiencing rapid growth across the United States." Competitions in the association's 17 regions culminate at the EXCA World Finals in Texas.

In Extreme Cowboy races, a course is set with approximately 10 obstacles, depending on the level of the class. The obstacles are billed as being challenging and require a trusting, well-trained horse and a relaxed and skilled rider. Obstacles may feature a ground-tying component, lead change, side-pass and speed, stop or rollback, in addition to conditions that simulate ranch work or trail riding.

FESTIVALS AND MORE

Cowboy Heritage Week

In British Columbia, Cowboy Heritage Week was first cele-brated in the East Kootenay from March 3 to 10, 2013. The occasion recognized the contributions made by cowboys and the ranching industry to the province's history, economy and culture. British Columbia has been home to a ranching industry for more than two centuries, but the year 2013 marked the first time this history was officially recognized by the provincial government.

DID YOU  KNOW?

The BC Cowboy Heritage Society oversees the Kamloops Cowboy Festival, the BC Cowboy Hall of Fame and the Joe Marten Memorial Award for the Preservation of Cowboy Heritage in BC. Their website also features a cowboy poetry page. You can visit the British Columbia Cowboy Heritage Society online at www.bcchs.com.

Kamloops Cowboy Festival

The annual Kamloops Cowboy Festival has gained a reputa-tion for being the largest festival of its kind in Canada and one of the largest in North America. It celebrates Kamloops' western heritage and showcases the best in cowboy poetry and western music, as well as featuring cowboy artists and artisans. The festival will celebrate its 18th anniversary in 2014.

Cowboy shooting events are popular in both Canada and the U.S.

Shoot 'Em Up

Cowboy action shooting events are held at various centers in Alberta, British Columbia, Saskatchewan and Washington State. Shooters compete in several classes, including cowboy, cowgirl, elder statesman and gunfighter. To find out when and where these events are held, check out www.rustywood. ca/rmr/schedule.html.

DID YOU  KNOW?

Every year, the BC Cowboy Heritage Society puts on a Cowboy Christmas Concert in Kamloops that is a fundraiser for the BC Cowboy Hall of Fame and the Kamloops Food Bank.

O'Keefe Ranch Cowboy Festival

Every summer, the Cowboy Festival is held over the August Heritage Day long weekend at the O'Keefe Ranch near Vernon,

British Columbia, where working cowboy and their trusty horses demonstrate their skills. Teams of cowboys from ranches all across the province converge on the O'Keefe Ranch to compete in the Ranch Rodeo, which highlights the working relationship between horse and rider that has been a part of ranching in British Columbia since the 1860s, when the O'Keefe Ranch was young. Spectators at the Ranch Rodeo can't help but be impressed by the incredible partnership between the cowboys and their horses.

Canadian Western Agribition

The Canadian Western Agribition, held in the provincial capital of Regina, features Saskatchewan's premier western exhibition and rodeo at the Brandt Centre. Over 100 of the toughest cowboys and cowgirls compete for the Canadian Cowboys' Association Championship, cash and prizes in this annual event. Canada's Farm Progress Show, also held annually in Regina and billed as being "as much about implements and new technology as it is about ranching," is Canada's largest farming tradeshow.

Awesome

The Canadian Western Agribition was honored as Event of the Year (Budget Over $20,000) at the Saskatchewan Tourism Awards of Excellence Gala, which was celebrated in Regina on April 25, 2013, at the Conexus Arts Centre.

Calgary Stampede Cowboy Up Challenge

The Calgary Stampede Cowboy Up Challenge is a multi-faceted equestrian sporting event that showcases both horse and rider as they maneuver through a series of obstacles, demonstrating both amazing horsemanship skills and incredible speed.

DID YOU  KNOW?

Both the Burgess Ranch, located in the Big Muddy region of southern Saskatchewan, and the Sturgeon River Ranch, on the west side of Prince Albert National Park, have hosted the popular Canadian TV series *Mantracker*. Filming took place for individual episodes at both locations.

Awesome

Canada's Farm Progress Show has been recognized as Canada's largest tradeshow, winning the Trade Show News Network Award for the third year in a row in 2013.

Cowboy Capital of the World

The town of Bandera, Texas, bills itself as the "Cowboy Capital of the World" and features monthly events ranging from cowgirl roundups, wild game dinners and classic car nights to cowboy music.

Cowboy Christmas Gift Show

The Cowboy Christmas Gift Show, billed as the longest running and the only "original" gift show of the Wrangler National Finals Rodeo, is held annually in Las Vegas. It has enough wares to keep even the most avid shopper entertained for the entire 10-day rodeo.

Florida Ranch Rodeo and Cowboy Heritage Festival

In 2013, the sixth annual Florida Ranch Rodeo and Cowboy Heritage Festival was called a rousing success as thousands of guests packed the Silver Spurs Arena in Kissimmee for two days of cowboy fun. Sixteen teams of cowboys and cowgirls from working ranches throughout Florida earned the right to compete in the Statewide Ranch Rodeo Finals by winning one of the regional ranch rodeos held throughout the state.

Canada's Greatest Working Cowboy

Lakeland College in Vermilion, Alberta, holds an annual competition to crown Canada's Greatest Working Cowboy, a testament to the winner's horsemanship and overall cowboy abilities. Contestants in the competition have points from at least three events totaled to see which cowboy has the greatest range of skills in a working environment. Five events are featured, including ranch roping, a stock dog trial, ranch doctoring, a ranch horse competition and bronc riding.

National Day of the American Cowboy

The National Day of the American Cowboy campaign was founded by *American Cowboy* magazine in 2004 "to preserve, protect and promote American cowboy and western heritage and to lobby for the passage of a national resolution designating the fourth Saturday of every July a permanent annual celebration honoring cowboys and cowgirls for their enduring contribution to the courageous, pioneering spirit of America."

COWBOY ART

Cowboy art runs the gamut from paintings and posters to sculptures, with common themes being cowboys, horses and picturesque western landscapes. Cowgirls are also often featured, as well as a lot of revolvers, cowboy apparel and events. A lot of commercial artwork features famous western movie stars like John Wayne and Clint Eastwood.

Traditional Cowboy Arts Association

According to its mission statement, the Traditional Cowboy Arts Association (TCAA) in the United States "is dedicated to preserving and promoting saddle making, bit and spur making, silversmithing and rawhide braiding, and the role of these traditional crafts in the cowboy culture of the American West." Founded in 1998, the association hopes to spark continuing interest in the four above-mentioned disciplines among members of the younger generation in the hope of keeping these skills alive. The National Cowboy and Western Heritage Museum in Oklahoma City hosts an annual exhibition and sale for the TCAA, and collaborates with them to put on workshops and seminars.

Cowboy Artists of America

The Cowboy Artists of America was founded in 1965 by four well-known American artists—Joe Beeler, Charlie Dye, John Hampton and George Phippen—with the mission "to authentically preserve and perpetuate the culture of western life in fine art."

Facebook Cowboy Art Sites

Facebook features several cowboy art sites, including the following:

- Cowboy Art Lovers
- Art of the American Cowboy
- Art of the Cowboy Makers

Artists in Canada

Artists in Canada features a variety of Canadian artists in the media of watercolors, oil paintings, acrylic paintings and sculpture. Their website (www.artistsincanada.com) lists a number of western artists who "paint a wide variety of artwork ranging from native art to cowboy art, horse portraits to human portraits." This appears to be an excellent forum for marketing western artists and their works.

Canadian Cutting Horses

Canadian Cutting Horses hosts a website (www.canadian-cuttinghorses.com) that bills itself as follows: "These western artists and cowboy artists paint a wide variety of artwork ranging from native art to cowboy art, cartoons, caricatures, art murals, horse portraits, Canadian scenery, the realistic and the imaginary." They promise to provide exposure for western artists looking to reach a wider audience.

Art Auctions

There are western art auctions such as Altermann Galleries & Auctioneers in Santa Fe, New Mexico, which listed celebrated art by well-known cowboy artists. In November 2013, they featured *Old Blue in the Lead* by Charlie Dye, which had an estimated price of $70,000 to $90,000.

COWBOY ARTISTS

There have been several giants among cowboy artists whose works are displayed in museums around the world in addition to many great contemporary cowboy artists.

Charles Russell, 1907

Charles Marion Russell (1864–1926)

One of the most famous of all artists of the Old West, Charles Marion "Kid" Russell is probably best known as "the cowboy artist." Born in Missouri, Russell enjoyed sketching and reading about the West as a child. He left school to work as a cowboy in Montana in 1880 and documented his experiences in watercolors. He left the outdoor life in 1892 and settled in Great Falls, Montana, to become a full-time artist.

The C.M. Russell Museum Complex in Great Falls, Montana, houses more than 2000 of Russell's artworks, personal objects and artifacts. Many of his works have sold for millions of dollars, and his 1918 painting *Piegans* went for a staggering $5.6 million at a 2005 auction.

DID YOU KNOW?

Russell created more than 2000 paintings of cowboys, Native Americans and landscapes set in the western U.S. and in Alberta, Canada, in addition to bronze sculptures. Russell was also a storyteller and author.

Charlie Dye (1906–73)

One of the founders of the Cowboy Artists of America, Charlie Dye was said to have had two natural affinities—he was good with horses and he could draw. Like the famed western artist Charles Russell, Dye spent much of his time as a working cowboy, but he also played semi-pro football and once worked as a bodyguard. He acquired his formal art training in Chicago and went on to work as a magazine illustrator before becoming a western artist. Although his paintings showcase a variety of western themes, his passion was for depicting the life of the working cowboy.

George Catlin (1796–1872)

Sometimes referred to as western artist, Catlin was a noted American painter, author and traveler who specialized in portraits of Native Americans in the Old West.

George Phippen (1915–66)

A western artist from Skull Valley, Arizona, George Phippen was a co-founder and the first president of the Cowboy Artists of America. A painter and sculptor, he produced approximately 3000 works in his 20-year career.

Geronimo and His Band Returning from a Raid in Mexico, 1888, by Frederic Remington for *Harper's Weekly*

Frederic Sackrider Remington (1861–1909)

Frederic Remington was regarded as the most prominent western artist at the turn of the 20th century, and other western artists back in the day, such as the famous Charles Russell, were considered members of the "School of Remington." (Clara Bascomb Sackrider was the name of Remington's mother, which explains his unusual middle name.) Remington's subjects often included cowboys, Native Americans and the U.S. Cavalry. He was not only an outstanding and prolific western artist, but also an accomplished correspondent, illustrator and author. Sadly, he died after an emergency appendectomy on December 26, 1909, led to peritonitis. His extreme obesity (he weighed nearly 300 pounds) complicated the anesthesia and surgery, and chronic appendicitis was cited in the post-mortem examination as an underlying factor in his death.

DID YOU  KNOW?

In 1886, Remington was sent to Arizona by *Harper's Weekly* magazine on commission as an artist-correspondent to cover the government's war against the feared Apache leader Geronimo. However, Remington never managed to meet the famed Native American chief.

COWBOY POETRY

It may sound a bit odd, but poetry is a big thing among a lot of cowboys, has been for years and is showing no signs of slowing down. There are dozens of associations for cowboy poets and singers in Canada and the United States. You just never know when you're going to run into a cowboy poet. Who would have thought that John Gattey of the celebrated Cross Bar Ranch near Consort, Alberta, would be a polished cowboy poet? Just ask him to recite, "It tastes like chicken," and you're in for a treat. Not to mention Don Brestler of Twin Butte, Alberta, who's a noted cowboy singer and artist. It seems that there's just no end of literary talent on the range, so to speak.

The Origins of Cowboy Poetry

Cowboy poetry is a unique poetic form rooted in cattle drives and working ranches. After a hard day's work, cowboys would gather around a campfire and entertain each other with stories—often tall tales—and songs. Because many cowboys were illiterate back in the day, poetic forms were employed to aid memory.

Poetry Associations and Gatherings

Nowadays, cowboy poets get together annually to share their poems about cowboys, horses and life on the range at some of the following places and events:

 Established in 1987, the Alberta Cowboy Poetry Association was created to promote and preserve Alberta's western heritage and traditions through poetry, music and storytelling. Members of all ages are encouraged to participate in the organization's events.

- The Stony Plain Cowboy Gathering Society, a not-for-profit organization, is made up of dedicated volunteers committed to the "preservation and presentation of historical and contemporary Cowboy Music, Poetry and Art." Stony Plain is located just west of Edmonton, Alberta. In 2013, the society hosted the 21st annual edition of this now legendary gathering.

- The Pincher Creek Cowboy Gathering, held in Pincher Creek, Alberta, has been celebrating music and poetry in the cowboy tradition since 1988 and marked its 26th anniversary in 2013.

- The Cowboy Poetry Gathering and Western Art and Gear Show in Maple Creek, Saskatchewan, celebrated its 24th anniversary in 2013. This three-day event, held in September, features participants from all over western Canada, as well as a few from the U.S.

- The Kamloops Cowboy Festival, sponsored by the BC Cowboy Heritage Society, will celebrate its 18th anniversary in March 2014.

- The Arizona Cowboy Poets Gathering had its 26th annual gathering at Prescott, Arizona, in 2013. Its focus is on maintaining the "true 'working cowboy' culture and heritage."

- Although cowboy poetry gatherings exist in almost all the western states as well as western Canada, the mother of them all is the annual National Cowboy Poetry Gathering held in Elko, Nevada. This event dates back to 1985.

Poetry and Music on the Web

There are several websites that feature cowboy poetry and music:

- 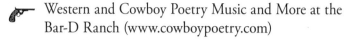 Western and Cowboy Poetry Music and More at the Bar-D Ranch (www.cowboypoetry.com)

- 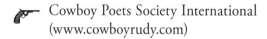 Western and Cowboy Poetry by Clark Crouch (poetry.crouchnet.com/western.html)

- Cowboy Poets Society International (www.cowboyrudy.com)

DID YOU KNOW?

Alberta's Robbie Robertson, who's also known as the "Mountie Cowboy Poet," has been associated with the Royal Canadian Mounted Police for more than 60 years and was an active member for 28 years. He writes and recites poetry about the early history of the force and some of its heroes, as well as writing and performing traditional cowboy poetry. He was the first member of the force to be given permission to wear the uniform after retirement for other than state or formal occasions. He wears either an 1895 NWMP period uniform or the current RCMP dress red serge while reciting his Mountie poetry.

COWBOY MUSIC

Cowboy Songs

A cowboy song is a song by or about cowboys, or both, and can be classified into two types. The first type is a song that is made up and passed on by word of mouth in the oral tradition. The second type of cowboy song is an adaptation of existing lyrics to a familiar tune, creating a new song in the process. The earliest collections of cowboy songs are credited to Nathan Howard Thorp, whose compilation, *Songs of the Cowboys*, published in 1908, is considered to be the first of its kind, and to John Avery Lomax, whose 1910 *Cowboy Songs and Other Frontier Ballads* gathered for the first time many songs that are now among the best known of the genre.

The Classics

There's obviously a lot of history behind cowboy songs, and some date back many years. "The Old Chisholm Trail" dates back to the 1870s and was one of the most popular songs sung by cowboys at the time. It is anecdotal, with each stanza detailing the typical ups and downs in the life of a cowboy. Tex Ritter and Randy Travis have both recorded "The Old Chisholm Trail."

"Git Along Little Dogies," which tells the story of the life of an old cowpuncher on the trail, was recorded by Roy Rogers in 1940 and is definitely a cowboy classic.

 COWBOY WISDOM

"Any cowboy can carry a tune. The trouble comes when he tries to unload it."

Singing around the campfire

Singing and Strumming

The classical cowboy musical instrument has nearly always been a guitar, with chords being strummed in a steady rhythm and likely followed by a fiddle, to kick off country dances. Cowboy music fans have many fond memories of songs that feature understandable lyrics and music with a toe-tapping rhythm.

Cowboy vs. Country Music

"Cowboy music" is distinct from what's called "country music," which is a genre of popular music that has its origins in rural America dating back to the 1920s and arising from both folk music and western music. Country music often combines ballads and dance melodies with simple harmonies, usually accompanied by string instruments (e.g. banjos, electric and acoustic guitars, fiddles), which provide a solid rhythm. Many country singers, of course, are backed up by a band with a drummer, piano player and guitarists. There may also be a harmonica in the mix.

Country music encompassed western music in the 1950s, and then jointly became known as country and western music. There are lots of famous country singers from Canada and the U.S., too many to outline in this book in any detail.

DID YOU KNOW?

Fiddles differ from violins in that they feature steel strings; however, the main thing that makes a fiddle a fiddle and a violin a violin is the type of music that is played on it. Generally, fiddlers play folk and traditional genres (e.g., Cajun or Celtic music) and violinists play composition-based (e.g., classical) music. Another difference is the technique used, though this isn't always consistent—a violin is held under the chin, whereas a fiddle is sometimes pressed into the front of the shoulder.

The Hit List

The Western Writers of America surveyed its members for the top 100 western songs of all time. The following top 10 are an interesting mixture of old, traditional songs, melodies from Hollywood movies and songs that many might label "country," which some folks actually consider one and the same with cowboy songs:

1. "(Ghost) Riders in the Sky: A Cowboy Legend": This is probably the most popular of all cowboy songs and owes its origins to cowboy poetry. Usually simply titled "Ghost Riders in the Sky," this song tells a folktale of a cowboy who has a vision of red-eyed, steel-hooved cattle thundering across the sky, being chased by the spirits of damned cowboys. He is warned that if he doesn't change his ways, he will become one of the ghostly riders. It was written in 1948 by Stan Jones and has been sung and played by more than 50 performers, including some of the best western singers and musicians such as Johnny Cash, Frankie Lane, The Outlaws and Duane Eddy, with the original score credited to Burl Ives.

2. "El Paso": This country and western ballad was written and originally recorded by Marty Robbins in 1959. It won the Grammy Award for Best Country and Western Recording in 1961.

3. "Cool Water": Written by Bob Nolan in 1936, this is a song about a man, his mule named Dan and a mirage in the desert. The best-known recording was done by Vaughn Monroe and the Sons of the Pioneers in 1948, but it has also been recorded by Hank Williams, Marty Robbins, Burl Ives, Johnny Cash and several other artists.

4. "The Streets of Laredo": This song, also known as "The Cowboy's Lament," can be traced back to the English folk song "The Unfortunate Rake." It is about a dying cowboy who tells his story to another cowboy who is passing by. A country music standard, it has been

COWBOY POETRY AND MUSIC

recorded and adapted numerous times, with many variations. The title refers to Laredo, Texas.

5. "Back in the Saddle Again": This was Gene Autry's signature song. It was co-written by Autry with Ray Whitley, first released in 1939 and inducted into the Grammy Hall of Fame in 1997.

6. "The Ballad of High Noon (Do Not Forsake Me, O My Darlin')": The theme song for the movie *High Noon*, this melody won the Academy Award for Best Original song in 1952 and was performed for the Academy by Tex Ritter.

7. "Oh Shenandoah": This traditional American folk song is also known as just "Shenandoah" or "Across the Wide Missouri." Although its origin is uncertain, it dates back to at least the early 19th century.

8. "Tumbling Tumbleweeds": This iconic cowboy song was composed by Bob Nolan and made famous by Gene Autry's 1935 movie of the same name.

9. "Home on the Range": This song personifies all that is great about the life of a cowboy and is often performed at events and in concerts.

10. "Red River Valley": This song's origin is uncertain, but it has gone by different names depending on where it was sung. Canadian folklorist Edith Fowke has anecdotal evidence that the song was known in at least five Canadian provinces before 1896.

DID YOU KNOW?

The song "Ghost Riders in the Sky" inspired the Marvel Comics Old West character Carter Slade, the Ghost Rider, who first appeared in 1967.

Singing cowboys, Odell, Oregon, 1941

Singing Cowboys

A "singing cowboy" was a quintessential cowboy hero in early western films, especially those popular in the 1930s and '40s. The typical singing cowboy was clean-shaven and wore a white hat while expressing himself in song. The image of the singing cowboy was established in 1925 when Texan Carl T. Sprague recorded the first cowboy song, "When the Work's All Done This Fall."

There have been several famous singing cowboys, including John Wayne, Gene Autry, Roy Rogers and Tex Ritter. These particular singing cowboys were considered all-American heroes in their day. When you consider the image of America that Hollywood was trying to portray to the world at the time, it is little wonder that the most famous singing cowboys projected such a wholesome image.

DID YOU KNOW?

John Wayne, who plays the character Singin' Sandy Saunders in the western movie *Riders of Destiny* (1933), sang ominously about showdowns. Wayne wore a black hat in this role, uncharacteristic of his later attire, though he rode a white horse and had a guitar strapped across his shoulder in the opening scene. He is considered the second singing cowboy of films, though his real voice wasn't used in the movie and was dubbed instead. The first singing cowboy on the silver screen was Ken Maynard, who appeared in the 1929 film *The Wagon Master*.

Dottie West

Although not a singing cowgirl, groundbreaking country singer Dottie West was one of the sexiest female performers that country music had to offer. Her career started in the 1960s, and she helped open doors for other female performers such as Dolly Parton, Barbara Mandrell and Lynn Anderson. Throughout the 1960s, she had a string of hits, including "Here Comes My Baby," "Paper Mansions," "Country Girl" and "You're Not Easy to Forget." Her career continued on into the '70s with hit solo songs, but she also teamed up with superstar Kenny Rogers for a series of duets that topped the country music charts. Dottie died at 58 years of age on September 4, 1991, a few days after sustaining injuries in a car accident.

Canadian Country Music Icon

Long billed as "Canada's Country Gentleman," Tommy Hunter pioneered country music in Canada. *The Tommy Hunter Show* began as a CBC Radio program in 1960 and went on to replace *Country Hoedown* on CBC Television in 1965; the show ran on CBC until 1992. *The Tommy Hunter Show* theme song, "Travellin' Man," was probably every bit as popular as the old CBC *Hockey Night in Canada* theme song now featured on TSN.

In 1984, Tommy Hunter was inducted into the Canadian Country Music Hall of Fame and he was made a Member of the Order of Canada two years later. He has received three Canadian Juno Awards and one Gemini Award.
In 1990, he was given a place in the Country Music Hall of Fame's "Walkway of Stars." A street—Tommy Hunter Way—is named in his honor in his hometown of London, Ontario, and in 2005, he received the Gospel Music Association of Canada Lifetime Achievement Award.

Ian Tyson

Another very distinguished Canadian country singer-songwriter, Ian Tyson is probably best known for his song "Four Strong Winds," an all-time classic. It was selected as the "greatest Canadian song of all time" on CBC Radio in 2005.

Tyson was a rodeo rider in his late teens and early twenties, and he took up playing the guitar while recovering from an injury he sustained in a rodeo fall. At one time, he was one half of the duo Ian & Sylvia with his former wife. From 1971 to 1975, he hosted a national television program, *The Ian Tyson Show*, on CTV, which was based on the 1970–71 music show *Nashville North*, later titled *Nashville Now*.
In 1989, he was inducted into the Canadian Country Music

Ian Tyson, 2010

Hall of Fame, and he became a Member of the Order of
Canada in 1994. He makes his home on a ranch near
Longview, Alberta.

DID YOU  KNOW?

Testament to Ian Tyson's popularity, on April 5, 2013,
a recording of "Four Strong Winds" was played during
the funeral of former Alberta premier Ralph Klein as the

honor guard brought Klein's urn into the Jack Singer Concert Hall in Calgary, Alberta.

Canadian Roll Call

Over the years, many country singers have made Canada proud, including Paul Brandt, George Canyon, Terri Clark, Wilf Carter, Charlie Chamberlain, Dick Damron, George Fox, Ray Griff, Tim Hus, Susan Jacks, Chad Klinger, k.d. lang, Gordon Lightfoot, Rita MacNeil, Murray McLauchlin, Anne Murray, Marg Osburne, Ronnie Prophet, Jimmy Rankin, Johnny Reid, Ray St. Germain, Hank Snow, Lucille Starr and Shania Twain, among many others.

Pioneering American Performers

While there have been many famous country singers from the United States, two of the pioneer performers stand out in particular as trailblazers of the modern era of this genre: legendary country singer Hank Williams and Patsy Cline, who revolutionized the role of women in country music.

Hank Williams

Hank Williams is widely regarded as one of the most significant country music artists of all time. He recorded 35 singles (five were released posthumously) that placed in the top 10 of the Billboard Country & Western Best Sellers chart, including 11 that ranked number one. In 1949, he released a cover of "Lovesick Blues," which carried him into the mainstream of country music. Among the hits he wrote were "Your Cheatin' Heart," "Hey, Good Lookin'" and "I'm So Lonesome I Could Cry." After an initial rejection, Williams joined the Grand Ole Opry, considered the epitomy of success for a country singer. Hank Williams died on New Year's Day in 1953 at the age of 29 from heart failure exacerbated by pills and alcohol.

DID YOU KNOW?

Hank Williams had 11 number one songs between 1948 and 1953, though he was unable to read or notate music to any significant degree. "Hey, Good Lookin'," one of the timeless classics that he penned, is considered his best song. It was a number one hit in 1951 and remains popular to this day. Several artists have covered the song, and it has joined some of his other classics in the Grammy Song Hall of Fame.

Patsy Cline

Virginia Patterson Hensley, known professionally as Patsy Cline, was an immensely popular American country music singer and a country music trailblazer. As an item in the early 1960s Nashville sound, Cline transitioned to a successful pop (and gospel) music career. She died an untimely death at age 30 in a private plane crash, when she was at the height of her career. Without doubt, she was one of the most influential, successful and acclaimed female vocalists of the 20th century. "Leavin' on Your Mind," "Crazy" and "I Fall to Pieces" were some of her greatest hits.

DID YOU KNOW?

Bill Peer, Hensley's second manager, gave her the name Patsy. She took her stage surname from her first husband, Gerald Cline.

American Roll Call

There have been a great many other outstanding country singers from the United States, including Eddy Arnold, Garth Brooks, Johnny Cash, the Carter Family, Glen Campbell,

Merle Haggard, Waylon Jennings, George Jones, Loretta Lynn, Tim McGraw, Reba McEntire, Ronnie Milsap, Willie Nelson, Buck Owens, Dolly Parton, Jim Reeves, Marty Robbins, Kenny Rogers, Ray Price, Charlie Pride, George Strait, Taylor Swift, Ernest Tubb, Dottie West, Tammy Wynette and Conway Twitty, among many others.

HOME ON THE RANGE

The Original Cowboy Song

Considered the unofficial anthem of the American West, "Home on the Range" is an iconic song that personifies the nostalgic life of a cowboy and his love of wide-open rangelands. Dr. Brewster M. Higley (1823–1911) originally wrote the words as a poem called "My Western Home" in the early 1870s in Smith County, Kansas. The poem was subsequently published in the December 1873 issue of the *Smith County Pioneer* under the title "Oh, Give Me a Home Where the Buffalo Roam." The music was written by Daniel E. Kelley, a friend of Higley. Higley's original words are similar to those of today, but not identical. There have been three major versions of the song over the years—the original by Higley (1876), one by William and Mary Goodwin (1904) and another by John A. Lomax (1910).

DID YOU  KNOW?

"Home on the Range" is the state song of Kansas and was featured as the state slogan on its vanity license plates in 2005. Today, the slogan on Kansas' license plates is "America's Heartland."

PARTNER DANCES

Country and western dance can be broken into two categories: partner dances and group dances. Partner dances include both "lead-and-follow dances," in which one partner leads and the other follows, and "pattern dances." Group dances include line dances and square dances. Country and western partner dances encompass several forms and styles of dance. They are stylistically associated both with American country and western and European traditions, and include the two-step, polka, swing and waltz.

Two-step

A two-step consists of two steps in the same direction with the same foot, separated by a closing step with the other foot. For example, a right two-step forward is a forward step onto the right foot, a closing step with the left foot, and then another forward step onto the right foot. The closing step may be done directly beside the other foot or even cross over, as long as the closing foot does not go past the other foot. The two-step is danced to medium- to fast-tempo country music in a pattern that progresses around the room.

The country two-step is danced to music with a $\frac{4}{4}$ beat that is usually heavy and easy to pick up. The count for the dance is slow, slow, quick, quick, with two beats for each slow step and one beat for each quick step. In modern times, this is known as the Texas two-step or Texas polka. There are many variations of the two-step that go back in time and have their roots in Europe.

Country and western dances remain popular to this day.

Polka

Polka is a genre of dance music that's very familiar throughout Europe and the Americas. It originated in the mid 19th century in Bohemia (the present-day Czech Republic) and later became popular at country and western dances in the U.S. and Canada. The polka is a lively dance for practiced partners with a flair for animation on the dance floor. This quick-paced dance features three steps and a hop. To recognize the music, listen for a fast-paced tune with four counts to the measure. The origin of the word "polka" may come from one or both of two sources. It may be named for the Poles who lived in southern Hungary—in Polish, the word *polka* means "Polish woman." On the other hand, polka may come from the Bohemian word *pulka*, which means "half," referring to the little half-step, or close step (i.e., hold), that's characteristic of this dance.

Swing

The country and western swing dance has roots in the culture of emancipated African Americans, but the most important influence came from cowboys themselves, who weren't held to any particular traditional dance conventions. Swing is an all-American couples rhythm dance consisting primarily of six- and eight-beat patterns that cover either a circular or slotted area on the dance floor. It incorporates the use of underarm turns, side passes, push breaks and whips, as well as four-beat rhythm breaks, syncopations and extensions of the same. There are many versions of the swing dance that evolved from the swing style of jazz music from the 1920s to the '50s.

Waltz

The waltz is a smooth, romantic, traditional, partnered ball-room and folk dance, known for its three-beat count (i.e., to the rhythm of "one-two-three"). It originated in central Europe and now has many variations from country to country. The country and western waltz is mostly progressive, moving counterclockwise around the dance floor. Both the posture and frame are relaxed, and the exaggerated hand and arm gestures of some ballroom styles are not part of this style. The waltz is usually interspersed with other dance forms during a night on the dance floor and is traditionally the very last dance of the evening.

DID YOU KNOW?

"The Tennessee Waltz," with music by Pee Wee King and lyrics by Redd Stewart, is one of the most popular country music songs ever recorded. It was written in 1946 and first released in December 1947 as a single by Cowboy Copas. "The Tennessee Waltz" became a multimillion-seller when Patti Page recorded it in 1950, and it was her biggest hit. The song was also recorded by Patsy Cline, among others.

GROUP DANCES

Line Dances

Line dances are popular in country and western dance bars and are a great way to get everyone on the dance floor. A country and western line dance features a choreographed, repetitive sequence of steps with a group of people dancing in one or more lines or rows (usually) without regard for gender. The dancers all face either each other or in the same direction, and everyone executes the steps at the same time. Line dancers are not (normally) in physical contact with each other, but there are some exceptions. Some line dances can take the form of a circle and are danced with partners. The common denominator for country and western line dancing is the ¼ meter, also known as "common time" (i.e., four beats, repeated).

Line dancing is similar to folk dancing and has grown in popularity since the early 1970s. Although there are many popular line dances, such as the Chicken Dance and the Macarena, the country and western line dancing genre has its own particular styles, for example, the "basic." The basic steps are as follows: move a foot, bring the other foot to match, move the first foot again, then bring the other foot to match again. Usually the dancers are in line and move together in fours or in eights. Overall directional movements are to the right, to the left, backward or forward, and can be done in straight lines, diagonal left or diagonal right. Up until recently, the most common move in line dances was the "Schottische," which is two side steps to the left and then to the right, followed by a turn in four steps. The country and western Crazy Foot Mambo, on the other hand, is a 32-count, four-wall, intermediate-level line dance.

DID YOU KNOW?

Some of the most popular country and western line dance songs include "Footloose," "Baby Likes to Rock It," "Country Girl (Shake It for Me)," "Honky Tonk Badonkadonk," "Save a Horse (Ride a Cowboy)," "Reggae Cowboy," "Dizzy," "Watermelon Crawl," "Boot Scootin' Boogie" and "Good Time."

Bow to your partner, a traditional square dance movement

Square Dance

A square dance is an old-time country and western dance for four couples (eight dancers) arranged in a square, with one couple on each side facing the middle of the square. There are two primary kinds of square dance music: hoedowns (for general patter calling) and singing calls (melodies that have words to go with them). "Turkey in the Straw" would be a good example of hoedown music, while "This Ole House" would fit well into the singing call category.

Traditional and modern square dancing have a number of calls in common, but there are usually small differences in the way they are performed. For example, the "allemande left" is traditionally performed by grasping left hands with another dancer, pulling away from each other slightly, walking halfway around a central axis, and then stepping through. In some square dances, "allemande left" can refer to a move in which two facing dancers take left hands or forearms, turn halfway around to the left, let go and step forward.

Larger dances sometimes request a strict western-style dress code, which originated in the late 1950s and early '60s, and is known as "traditional square dance attire" even though it was not traditional before that time.

Dance Tunes

"Turkey in the Straw" is a well-known American folk song that dates from the early 19th century. "This Ole House" (sometimes written as "This Old House") is a popular song written by Stuart Hamblen and published in 1954. It is sung in an upbeat manner despite the sadness of the lyrics and has been recorded by many artists including Wilf Carter, Carl Perkins and the Statler Brothers.

DID YOU KNOW?

The country and western square dance is one of the most widely known dance forms worldwide because of its association in the 20th century with the romanticized image of the American cowboy as popularized by Hollywood film producers. Consequently, square dancing is strongly associated with the U.S., as well as Canada. Nineteen states have designated it as their official state dance.

COWBOYS ON STAGE

Wild West shows were popular traveling vaudeville perfor-
mances in the U.S. and Europe. The original Wild West
show that defined this entertainment genre was Buffalo
Bill's, which began in 1883 and lasted until 1913. These
shows introduced many western performers and personali-
ties, and showcased a romanticized version of the Old
West for a wide audience. Famous cowboy performers
were celebrities back in the day and were notorious for
their riding and shooting skills and showmanship.

William Frederick "Buffalo Bill" Cody (1846–1917)

Buffalo Bill Cody was a Civil War Union scout, bison hunter
and showman who was widely regarded as an American folk
hero. He was born in the Iowa Territory (now the state of Iowa),
in Le Claire, then lived for several years in Canada before his
family moved to the Kansas Territory. Buffalo Bill received the
Medal of Honor in 1872 for service to the U.S. Army in
the 3rd Cavalry Regiment for "gallantry in action" while
serving as a civilian scout. However, the award was revoked
in 1917 because he was not a regular member of the armed
forces at the time. It was restored posthumously in 1989.

Buffalo Bill is regarded as one of the most colorful figures
of the American West and became famous for the shows he
organized with "cowboy and Indian" themes. His Wild West
shows toured in Great Britain and Europe, as well as the
United States. Cody's headline performers were celebrities
in their own right. For example, Annie Oakley and her
husband Frank Butler performed as sharpshooters together
with performers such as Gabriel Dumont and Lillian Smith.
Although Cody apparently made a fortune from his shows,

Buffalo Bill with Chief Sitting Bull, 1885

he lost most of it as a result of mismanagement and a weakness for dubious investment schemes. In the end, the Wild West show itself was lost to creditors.

Cody died on January 10, 1917, and is buried in a tomb blasted from solid rock at the summit of Lookout Mountain near Denver, Colorado.

DID YOU  KNOW?

In 1867, Cody started buffalo hunting to feed construction crews building railroads, which is where he got his nickname "Buffalo Bill." By his own reports, he killed 4280 bison in 17 months.

Wild West show perfomer Annie Oakley, circa 1899

Annie Oakley (1860–1926)

Annie Oakley, born Phoebe Ann Moses in Darke County, Ohio, was an American sharpshooter and exhibition shooter. Her awesome talent and notoriety led to a starring role in Buffalo Bill's Wild West Show, which rocketed her to fame as America's first female superstar.

Annie began trapping at a young age, and at age eight was shooting and hunting to support her siblings and her widowed mother. Traveling show marksman Francis E. "Frank" Butler, an Irish immigrant, placed a $100 bet with Cincinnati hotel owner Jack Frost in 1875, that he, Butler, could beat any local fancy shooter. The hotelier arranged a shooting match between Butler and the 15-year-old Annie. After missing on his 25th shot, Butler lost both the match and the bet. Soon he began courting Annie, and they married on August 23, 1876. They joined Buffalo Bill's Wild West Show in 1885.

Oakley, the stage name Annie adopted when she and Frank began performing together, is believed to have been taken from the neighborhood of Oakley, Cincinnati, where the couple resided after they married. Annie died on November 3, 1926, and Frank died three weeks later. They didn't have any children. Annie and Frank are buried in Greenville, Ohio, side by side. Both their tombstones say, "At Rest."

DID YOU  KNOW?

In 1935, actress Barbara Stanwyck played Annie Oakley in a fictionalized biographical film called *Annie Oakley*. There was also a fictionalized TV series called *Annie Oakley* that ran from 1954 to 1957. The 1946 Broadway musical *Annie Get Your Gun*, with lyrics and music by Irving Berlin, was a hit and had long runs in both New York (1147 performances) and London.

AWESOME

Annie Oakley's most incredible and famous trick was being able to repeatedly split a playing card that had been thrown into the air, edge-on, and put several more holes in it before it touched the ground, using a .22-caliber rifle at 90 feet (27 meters).

Gordon William "Pawnee Bill" Lillie (1860–1942)

Born Gordon William Lillie, Pawnee Bill was a world-renowned Wild West showman and performer, best known for his short partnership with Buffalo Bill Cody. Lillie was born in Bloomington, Illinois, but the family moved to Wellington, Kansas, while he was still a child. It was in Kansas that Lillie's lifelong relationship with the Pawnee people began, and by the age of 19, he was working for the Pawnee Indian Agency in Indian Territory (present-day Oklahoma). In 1883, he was recruited to work with Buffalo Bill's Wild West Show as a Pawnee interpreter. He married trick shooter and rider Mary "May" Manning in 1886, and the couple ran their own Wild West show from 1888 to 1908. A businessman as well as a showman, Pawnee Bill successfully invested in oil, real estate and banking. He and his wife were also instrumental in helping to preserve the endangered plains bison. Pawnee Bill died in his sleep on February 3, 1942.

Mary E. "May" Manning Lillie (1869–1936)

Mary "May" Manning, born in Philadelphia, Pennsylvania, was an American sharpshooter and rider. She married Gordon William Lillie (who became famous as Pawnee Bill) in 1886 at her parent's home in Philadelphia. Lillie's wedding gift to his bride was a pony and a Marlin .22-caliber target rifle. Two years after their wedding, they launched their own Wild West show, which they named Pawnee Bill's Historic Wild West. For 20 years, from 1888 to 1908, May and Bill traveled the country and entertained thousands. A crack shot, May was billed as the "Champion Girl Horseback Shot of the West." Eventually the couple settled in Pawnee, Oklahoma, on Blue Hawk Peak, where May became one of the first American women to raise plains bison. She died on September 17, 1936, from injuries sustained in a car accident.

DID YOU KNOW?

May quit the couple's show after Pawnee Bill shot a piece of her finger off during a trick performance that went wrong, and she ran the family's ranch instead. She also starred in her own movie, *May Lillie, Queen of the Buffalo Ranch.* On October 26, 2011, May Manning was inducted into the National Cowgirl Hall of Fame.

Lillian Smith (1871–1930)

Born in Coleville, California, trick shooter and trick rider Lillian Frances Smith joined Buffalo Bill's Wild West Show in 1886 at the age of 15 and was billed as the "Champion California Huntress"—a direct rival to Annie Oakley in the show. The two women were experts with different long guns: Oakley favored the shotgun, while Smith preferred the rifle. As rivals, she and Oakley were not always on good terms with each other. In contrast to the conservative Oakley, Smith was a braggart, enjoyed flashy clothing and had a reputation for being a shameless flirt, perhaps even promiscuous.

Smith left the show in 1889, and in 1907, she moved to Oklahoma to become a fixture with the Miller Brothers

101 Ranch Wild West Show. Smith performed as Princess Wenona, a fictionalized Sioux princess. She also continued to perform in other shows, including Pawnee Bill's. After another 13 years as a record-setting sharpshooter and performer, Smith retired around 1920.

DID YOU KNOW?

At the age of seven, Lillian became bored with dolls and asked her father for a "little rifle" instead. She performed in San Francisco at age 10, and soon her father offered a $5000 wager that no one could beat her. This was apparently not an idle boast because she challenged Doc Carver, one of the era's best-known marksmen, to a competition in St. Louis, and he never showed up.

Willie M. "Bill" Pickett (1870–1932)

Born in Jenks Branch in Travis County, Texas, in 1870, Bill Pickett (also known as the "Bulldogger") was a cowboy and rodeo performer who introduced bulldogging (steer wrestling) to the rodeo stage. Along with his four brothers, he established the Pickett Brothers Bronco Busters and Rough Riders Association. In 1905, Pickett joined the Miller Brothers 101 Ranch Wild West Show, which featured well-known celebrities such as Buffalo Bill Cody, Cowboy Bill Watts, Will Rogers, Tom Mix, Bee Ho Gray and Zach and Lucille Mulhall. He was billed as the "World's Colored Champion" and performed "death-defying feats of courage and skill." However, being an African American was a handicap that kept him out of some performances. Shortly after he retired from Wild West shows in 1932, Pickett was tragically killed when he was kicked in the head by a wild bronco. In 1971, he was inducted into the National Rodeo Cowboy Hall of Fame.

DID YOU KNOW?

Bill Pickett is credited with inventing the technique of bulldogging (now known as steer wrestling), which involves grabbing a steer by the horns, twisting the animal's neck and wrestling it to the ground. Cattlemen knew that a stray steer could be captured with the help of a trained bulldog, and Pickett thought that if a bulldog could do this feat, so could he. He practiced his stunt by riding hard and springing from his horse, then wrestling the steer to the ground.

Will Rogers (1879–1935)

Will Rogers, one of the world's most famous celebrities in the 1920s and 1930s, was born in Oologah, Indian Territory (present-day Oklahoma). His Wild West show act was a display of daring riding and clever tricks with his lariat, and he toured as a rider and trick roper in Texas Jack's Wild West Circus in South Africa and later with the Wirth Brothers Circus in Australia and New Zealand. He returned to the United States in 1904 to try his roping skills on the vaudeville circuits. Rogers' vaudeville rope act led to success in the Ziegfeld Follies, which in turn led to the first of his many movie contracts in both silent films and "talkies." He went on to become a journalist and radio broadcaster, as well as a political commentator—people loved his down-to-earth humor and intelligent observations. Rogers' life was cut short in a plane crash near Point Barrow, Alaska, on August 15, 1935.

Will Rogers (date unknown)

DID YOU  **KNOW?**

Will Rogers starred in 71 films and several Broadway shows and was voted the most popular male actor in Hollywood in 1934.

THE GOOD, THE BAD AND THE WORST

The Heyday of Cowboy Movies

The heyday of cowboy movies was in the 1950s and '60s. Many western flicks are considered classics, noted for straightforward good-versus-evil plots in the frontier days of the American Wild West. With the exception of newbie Clint Eastwood, most of these movies featured top-rated, established Hollywood actors. There are many outstanding western movies, and which ones are the best varies depending on the reviewer. Recent interest in western movies was spawned by the 2013 western film *The Lone Ranger*, produced by Walt Disney Pictures and Jerry Bruckheimer Films. It stars Johnny Depp as Tonto, the narrator of the events, and Armie Hammer as John Reid, the Lone Ranger.

 COWBOY WISDOM

"It is easier to get an actor to be a cowboy than to get a cowboy to be an actor."

The Good

In a July 5, 2013, *Edmonton Journal* article entitled "The cowboy movie hall of fame," Bob Thompson chronicled his take on classic western movies. His article featured the byline: "If you like the Lone Ranger here are 10 even better westerns." His list of favorites was as follows:

 The Good, the Bad and the Ugly (1966)

 Unforgiven (1992)

- *My Darling Clementine* (1946)
- *True Grit* (2010)
- *Butch Cassidy and the Sundance Kid* (1969)
- *The Searchers* (1956)
- *Red River* (1948)
- *Little Big Man* (1970)
- *The Westerner* (1940)
- *She Wore a Yellow Ribbon* (1949).

The Bad

Thompson also listed five cowboy movies to avoid at all costs:

- *Barbarosa* (1982)
- *Two Mules for Sister Sara* (1970)
- *The Quick and the Dead* (1995)
- *Legends of the Fall* (1994) and *Tombstone* (1993).

And the Worst

Online lists of lousy western movies rated the following among the worst:

- *Brothers in Arms* (2005)
- *The Quick and the Undead* (2006)
- *Jesse James Meets Frankenstein's Daughter* (1966)
- *Les Dalton* (2004)
- *The Terror of Tiny Town* (1938).

WESTERN MOVIE HALL OF FAME

While the films mentioned above are all great movies, I will offer my personal review of the all-time best ones based on ratings by other movie critics, box office sales, Academy Award nominations and awards, as well as other awards. There are also many other lists of the top western movies available online.

High Noon (1952)

High Noon is an outstanding 1952 western film directed by Fred Zinnemann and starring Gary Cooper and Grace Kelly. The plot's sequence of events occurs in real time and centers on William "Will" Kane (Gary Cooper), the longtime marshal of Hadleyville in New Mexico Territory, who has just married the beautiful and charming pacifist Quaker Amy Fowler (Grace Kelly) and turned in his badge. Kane intends to become a storekeeper elsewhere in the West. Suddenly, the townspeople learn that Frank Miller (Ian MacDonald), a criminal whom Kane brought to justice, is going to arrive on the noon train to settle a score with the former marshal. Kane is forced to face the killers alone when his would-be supporters abandon him. The film's theme song, "The Ballad of High Noon (Do Not Forsake Me, O My Darlin')," sets the stage for the showdown between Kane and Miller as the clock ticks toward high noon.

The film won four Academy Awards and two Golden Globes, a testament to just how great *High Noon* was in its day.

DID YOU  KNOW?

Producer Stanley Kramer first offered the leading role of Will Kane to Gregory Peck, who turned it down because he felt it was too similar to his part in *The Gunfighter*. Other actors who turned down the role of Will Kane include Charlton Heston, Marlon Brando, Kirk Douglas and Montgomery Clift.

Shane (1953)

Shane, a 1953 western from Paramount, stars Alan Ladd, an American film actor and one of the most popular and well-known celebrities of the 1940s and the first half of the 1950s. Ladd was one of Hollywood's most celebrated and handsome actors in his time—a James Dean of the day. *Shane* was produced and directed by George Stevens, and was based on a 1949 novel of the same name by Jack Schafer. Besides Ladd, the movie stars Jean Arthur (in the final role of her 30-year career) and Van Heflin, as well as Brandon de Wilde, Elisha Cook Jr., Jack Plalance and Ben Johnson.

The plot hinges on a stranger named "Shane," played by handsome Alan Ladd, who is garbed in buckskin with a revolver on his hip. He rides into an isolated part of Wyoming, befriends a homesteader named Joe Starrett (Van Heflin) and his family, and is drawn into a conflict between Starrett's family and a cruel cattle baron, Rufus Ryker (Emile Meyer), who wants to force Starrett and other homesteaders off their land. The movie features a classic western gunfight in which Shane kills Ryker's hired gunslinger, played by Jack Palance, and his gang of accomplices. The film was nominated for five Academy Awards, including Best Picture.

DID YOU KNOW?

Jack Palance is probably best remembered for his on-stage one-armed pushups four decades after his film debut in *Shane*, at the 1992 Academy Awards ceremony in which he won the award for Best Supporting Actor for his performance as cowboy Curly Washburn in the comedy western *City Slickers*. At the time he filmed *Shane*, Palance was not comfortable with horses.

Gunfight at the OK Corral (1957)

Gunfight at the OK Corral stars two of Hollywood's most famous actors of the 1950s, Burt Lancaster as Wyatt Earp and Kirk Douglas as Doc Holliday. John Sturges directed the film from a screenplay written by novelist Leon Uris.

The movie is based on a real event—a gunfight that took place at about 3:00 PM on Wednesday, October 26, 1881, in Tombstone, Arizona Territory. It is generally regarded as the most famous gunfight in the history of the Old West. However, the film is a rather loose Hollywood retelling of the event and makes no pretense at historical accuracy. The gunfight, thought to have lasted only about 30 seconds, was fought between outlaw cowboys Billy Claiborne, Ike and Billy Clanton, and Tom and Frank McLaury versus the town marshal, Virgil Earp, and his brothers Morgan Earp, the assistant town marshal, and temporary lawman Wyatt Earp. The Earps were aided by Doc Holliday, who had been designated a temporary marshal by Virgil.

The theme song for *Gunfight at the OK Corral* is all western and sets the mood for the infamous gunfight. A big hit in its day, the film earned $4.7 million on its first run and $6 million on re-release. It was also nominated for two Academy Awards.

DID YOU  KNOW?

Despite its historical name, the gunfight actually occurred in a narrow lot six doors west of the rear entrance to the OK Corral and also in the street. The two opposing parties were initially only about 6 feet (1.8 meters) apart. Approximately 30 shots were fired in 30 seconds. Ike Clanton filed murder charges against the Earps and Doc Holliday, but the Earps and Holliday were eventually exonerated by a local judge after a 30-day preliminary hearing and then again by a local grand jury.

The Big Country (1958)

The Big Country was directed by William Wyler and stars Gregory Peck, who also co-produced the film with Wyler. The all-star cast includes Jean Simmons, Carroll Baker, Charleton Heston, Burl Ives, Charles Bickford and Chuck Connors. The film is based on the serialized magazine novel *Ambush at Blanco Canyon* by Donald Hamilton. It was a big hit even though it has a complicated plot that centers on a feud between a large rancher and a poorer neighbor over water. Ives won the Academy Award for Best Supporting Actor, as well as a Golden Globe Award. The film was also nominated for an Academy Award for the musical score by Jerome Moross. The popular soundtrack is an American favorite.

DID YOU  KNOW?

Burl Ives recorded the original version of "Ghost Riders in the Sky," one of the most popular western songs ever, in 1949. He had numerous hit songs during his long and illustrious career.

The Man Who Shot Liberty Valance (1962)

This highly rated 1962 western was directed by John Ford and features two of the biggest Hollywood stars of the day, James Stewart and John Wayne. Ford had a reputation as being difficult to work with, though he did have a good relationship with Wayne. The movie also stars Vera Miles and Lee Marvin. Marvin plays the gunfighter Liberty Valance, the head of a gang of ruthless outlaws. The film was shot in black and white, which suits the somber mood of the plot. It was an instant hit when released in April 1962, owing in large part to its classic story and popular stars. Produced on a budget of $3.2 million, the film grossed $8 million at the box office, making it the 16th highest grossing film of 1962.

DID YOU  KNOW?

Burt Bacharach and Hal David later wrote a popular song entitled "The Man Who Shot Liberty Valance," based on the plotline of the movie. The song became a top 10 hit for singer Gene Pitney, but was not used in the film. Apparently, Pitney was not asked to record the song until after the film came out.

The Good, the Bad and the Ugly (1966)

Released in 1966, *The Good, the Bad and the Ugly* was the third installment in Sergio Leone's "spaghetti western" trilogy and followed *A Fistful of Dollars* (1964) and *For a Few Dollars More* (1965). The movie has one of the most memorable soundtracks, composed by Ennio Morricone, ever recorded in any flick.

The western stars a cocksure Clint Eastwood as the Man with No Name, with Lee Van Cleef as a despicable villain and Eli Wallach. The three actors play the roles of three very different cowboys during the U.S. Civil War. The plot revolves around these three gunslingers competing to find a fortune in buried Confederate gold amid the violent chaos of gunfights, hangings, Civil War battles and prison camps. Eastwood stars as Blondie, "the Good," a subdued bounty hunter. Lee Van Cleef is Angel Eyes, "the Bad," a ruthless, unfeeling, socio-pathic mercenary. Eli Wallach plays Tuco Ramírez, "the Ugly," a comical though very dangerous, fast-talking Mexican bandit who is wanted by the authorities for a long list of crimes.

Despite the original negative reception by some film critics, *The Good, the Bad and the Ugly* has since accumulated very positive feedback. Some critics consider it to be one of the best western films ever made, and it remains one of the most popular and well-known movies of the genre.

Spaghetti Westerns

The spaghetti western is a broad sub-genre of western films that emerged in the mid-1960s in the wake of Sergio Leone's movies, which were international box-office successes. The term was used by movie critics in the U.S. and other countries because most of these westerns were produced and directed by Italians. Leone, who shifted his attention from epic films to spaghetti westerns, was the Italian director, producer and screenwriter most associated with the genre, which owed its origins (and its heart) to the American western.

DID YOU KNOW?

Clint Eastwood got his start in show business as a supporting cast member in the TV series *Rawhide* (1959–66). He made famous the saying, "Go ahead, make my day," a catchphrase written by Charles B. Pierce and spoken by the character Harry Callahan in the 1983 film *Sudden Impact*. Eastwood rose to fame playing the Man with No Name in Sergio Leone's *Dollars* trilogy of spaghetti westerns (*A Fistful of Dollars, For a Few Dollar More* and *The Good, the Bad and the Ugly*) during the late 1960s.

The Wild Bunch (1969)

The Wild Bunch is an epic western film full of violence directed by Sam Peckinpah. It stars William Holden, Ernest Borgnine, Robert Ryan, Ben Johnson and Warren Oates. The plot centers on an aging outlaw gang on the Texas-Mexico border trying to exist in the changing world of 1913. After a failed payroll robbery, the Wild Bunch, led by aging outlaw Pike Bishop (William Holden) and including Dutch (Ernest Borgnine), Angel (Jaime Sanchez), and Lyle and Tector Gorch (Warren Oates and Ben Johnson), heads for Mexico pursued by the gang of Pike's friend-turned-nemesis, Deke Thornton (Robert Ryan). Caught between the corruption of railroad bigshot Harrigan (Albert Dekker) and Federale general Mapache (Emilio Fernandez) and without a frontier to escape to, the Wild Bunch opts for a final devastating shootout, striding purposefully to confront Mapache and avenge their friend Angel, ultimately to their demise.

The writing of Peckinpah, Walon Green and Roy N. Sickner was nominated for an Academy Award for Best Screenplay; Jerry Fielding's music was nominated for Best Original Score; Peckinpah was nominated for an Outstanding Directorial

Achievement Award by the Directors Guild of America; and cinematographer Lucien Ballard won the National Society of Film Critics Award for Best Cinematography.

Critics of *The Wild Bunch* noted the theme of the end of the outlaw gunfighter era. The film polarized movie critics and audiences over its ferocious bloodshed. The final, graphic shootout between the Wild Bunch and the Mexicans is a classic duster finale, but it is touching in a macabre way, as the last of the American outlaws pass on into history.

DID YOU KNOW?

The Wild Bunch is noted for its cutting-edge, multi-angle, quick-cut editing, which uses both normal and slow motion to depict violent imagery and gross bloodshed. The technique was revolutionary in 1969, and the violence is in stark contrast to Jerry Fielding's soothing soundtrack.

Butch Cassidy and the Sundance Kid (1969)

Butch Cassidy and the Sundance Kid is a highly entertaining film directed by George Roy Hill and written by William Goldman, who won the Academy Award for Best Original Screenplay for the film.

The plot is based loosely on fact and depicts the story of outlaws Robert LeRoy Parker, known historically as Butch Cassidy (Paul Newman), and his partner in crime Harry Longabaugh, the Sundance Kid (Robert Redford), as they migrate to Bolivia while on the run from the law. The action takes place in the late 1890s and starts in Wyoming, with Butch Cassidy as the affable leader of the outlaw Hole-in-the-Wall Gang. The movie has a humorous spin but a predictable ending, with a freeze-frame shot of Butch and Sundance charging out of a building they'd holed up in, guns blazing, as Bolivian forces fire on them.

The film received mixed reviews but earned $15 million in North America during its first year of release. With U.S. box office returns of over $100 million, it was the top-grossing film of 1969 and also won four Academy Awards.

DID YOU  KNOW?

The more commonly used name for Butch Cassidy and the Sundance Kid's outlaw gang was the Wild Bunch. However, when the Sam Peckinpah film *The Wild Bunch* was released a few months earlier, the name of Butch and Sundance's gang was changed to the Hole-in-the-Wall Gang to avoid confusion with Peckinpah's film.

Little Big Man (1970)

Little Big Man is an anti-establishment western directed by Arthur Penn and based on the 1964 novel by Thomas Berger. The movie stars Dustin Hoffman, Chief Dan George, Faye Dunaway, Martin Balsam, Jeff Corey and Richard Mulligan. It's a darkly satirical comedy about a white boy raised by the Cheyenne Nation during the 19th century. The film tells a rather sad story about the contrasting lives of pioneers and Native Americans throughout the progression of the boy's life to manhood and then to old age. Native Americans receive a more sympathetic treatment than do U.S. Cavalry soldiers, who are depicted as villains. A scene showing the cavalry massacring Native American women and children is particularly disturbing. Despite its satiric approach, the film has tragic elements and a clear social conscience about prejudice and injustice. It is a prime example of anti-establishment movies of the period, protesting America's involvement in the Vietnam War by portraying the U.S. military negatively.

The plot features 121-year-old Jack Crabb (Dustin Hoffman), who recounts his colorful life story to a curious historian (William Hickey). Among other things, Crabb had been a captive of the Cheyenne, a gunslinger, an associate of Wild Bill Hickok (Jeff Corey) and a scout for General George Armstrong Custer (Richard Mulligan).

Little Big Man received widespread acclaim from film critics. Chief Dan George was nominated for an Academy Award for Best Actor in a Supporting Role, and won many honors for his performance.

DID YOU KNOW?

In order to get the raspy voice of a man who is supposed to be 121 years old, Hoffman sat in his dressing room and screamed at the top of his lungs for an hour before going in front of the cameras. The historical Little Big Man was actually a Native American leader who bore no resemblance to the Jack Crabb character in the movie. Little Big Man was known for his involvement in the capture and possible assassination of Crazy Horse at Fort Robinson in 1877. He also fought at the Battle of the Little Big Horn, a conflict that is depicted in the film.

Dances with Wolves (1990)

Dances with Wolves, directed, produced by and starring Kevin Costner, received widespread acclaim by movie critics. It features a great story with excellent actors and superior directing. Adapted from a 1988 book of the same name by Michael Blake, the movie tells the story of First Lieutenant

John Dunbar (Costner), a heroic Union Army officer. After the Civil War, Dunbar requests a post on the American frontier, and the film depicts his encounter and evolving relationship with the Lakota people. The movie was shot in South Dakota and Wyoming and features beautiful scenery.

Dances with Wolves won seven Academy Awards, including Best Picture and Best Director, as well as the Golden Globe Award for Best Motion Picture–Drama. The fact that it won so many Academy Awards is testament to it being one of the best films ever.

DID YOU KNOW?

Kevin Costner developed the film over a period of five years, with an initial budget of $15 million. Because of budget overruns and general industry reluctance to invest in a western movie, Costner was forced to personally make up the rest of the film's $18 million budget. The project went on to gross over $100 million, so Costner earned an estimated $40 million from his original investment.

3:10 to Yuma (1957, 2007)

The 2007 version of *3:10 to Yuma* is not just another remake, and some critics feel it exceeds the original 1957 movie, which was directed by Delmer Daves and starred Glenn Ford and Van Heflin. The earlier movie was well received on release and is still highly regarded today, largely on the strength of its cast and plot. The captivating title song for the 1957 film, "The 3:10 to Yuma," was sung by Frankie Laine.

The 2007 film stars Christian Bale and Russell Crowe, who plays a very different role than is usual for him—the ruthless villain Ben Wade. When Dan Evans (Christian Bale) and his boys happen upon a train robbery led by Wade, their paths become hopelessly intertwined. Evans is a man of conviction with a strong moral code and decides to join a posse that is taking the captured Wade to town to put him on the 3:10 train to Yuma. However, Wade's gang, led by the equally ruthless Charlie Prince (Ben Foster), surrounds the posse in an attempt to free Wade before he is put on the train.

Both film versions have a great script and a fast-moving plot.

DID YOU  KNOW?

Canadian-born Glenn Ford began his film career in 1937. His first western was *Texas* (1941), and he made more than two dozen westerns in his nearly 60-year career, as well as a number of western television movies and series. Ford was inducted into the Hall of Fame of Great Western Performers at the National Cowboy and Western Heritage Museum in 1978. He was also credited with being the fastest gun in Hollywood, able to draw and fire in less than half a second, making him faster than such western entertainment legends as James Arness and John Wayne.

True Grit (2010)

Written and directed by the Coen brothers, the 2010 film *True Grit* is the second adaptation of Charles Portis' 1968 novel of the same name. The earlier version was filmed in 1969 and starred John Wayne and Glenn Campbell.

The plot features a tough U.S. marshal who helps a stubborn young woman track down her father's murderer. The 2010 film stars Hailee Steinfeld as Mattie Ross, whose father is murdered by one of his hired hands, Tom Chaney (Josh Brolin), when Mattie is 14 years old. Mattie hires U.S. marshal

Reuben "Rooster" J. Cogburn (Jeff Bridges), to track down her father's killer.

The film is probably one of the last great western movies produced up until the present time. Although it was nominated for 10 Academy Awards, it won none.

DID YOU KNOW?

The original 1969 *True Grit* starred John Wayne as Reuben "Rooster" J. Cogburn, a drunken, hard-nosed U.S. marshal and bounty hunter, and Glenn Campbell as Texas Ranger LaBoeuf (played by Matt Damon in the 2010 version). John Wayne won an Academy Award for Best Actor for his performance in the film.

A CANADIAN TWIST

There are relatively few Canadian "western" movies, per se, probably because the pattern of Canada's settlement was founded on the basis of law and order brought forward by the North-West Mounted Police in response to American whiskey traders in southern Alberta.

The Englishman's Boy (2008)

The most recent Canadian western movie, *The Englishman's Boy*, premiered as a made-for-television film on CBC in 2008. The film is based on a 1996 novel by Guy Vanderhaeghe, which won the Governor General's Award for English language fiction and was nominated for the Giller Prize. It deals with the events of the 1873 Cypress Hills Massacre as told 50 years later to a young screenwriter in Hollywood by the last living survivor. It is a telling story of life on the frontier in Montana and western Canada prior to settlement.

Northern Westerns

The "northern western" or "northwestern" genre, as compared with the classic "western" genre, is a North American literature and film genre popularized by authors such as Rex Beach, Zane Grey, Jack London, Robert Service and James Oliver Curwood. Plots are based on tales from the Canadian North and typically feature straitlaced, stereotyped Mounties instead of cowboys, as well as Native Americans, U.S. marshals and sheriffs and the American cavalry, the latter sometimes cast in a seedy light. The genre was popular between the two world wars.

The films are set in western Canada and contrast the law and order in Canada with the lawless American West. For example, in the movies *Pony Soldier* (1952) and *Saskatchewan* (1954), the North-West Mounted Police come across as being fair and compassionate in their dealings with Native peoples as opposed to Hollywood's portrayal of the oftentimes ruthless soldiers of the U.S. Cavalry, who murdered defenseless Native American women and children.

DID YOU KNOW?

Pony Soldier is a 1952 northern western set in Canada but filmed in Sedona, Arizona. Starring Tyrone Power, a Hollywood giant in his day, the film is based on a 1951 *Saturday Evening Post* story by Garnett Weston entitled "Mounted Patrol." Set in 1876, the film deals with North-West Mounted Police constable Duncan MacDonald, recently posted to Fort Walsh in the Cypress Hills, who is tasked with freeing two hostages being held by the Cree.

URBAN COWBOY MOVIE AND MOVEMENT

The Movie

Urban Cowboy is a 1980 American western romance-drama about the love-hate relationship between Buford "Bud" Davis, played by John Travolta, and Sissy Davis, played by Debra Winger. The film is said to have started the 1980s boom in pop-country music known as the "Urban Cowboy movement," also called "neo-country" or "hill boogie." The movie was filmed in Houston, Huntsville and Pasadena, Texas, as well as in Pico Rivera, California.

Mechanical Bull Riding

The movie's centerpiece was a mechanical bull ride in Gilley's nightclub, a contest that becomes the focus of the rivalry between Travolta's character, Bud, and Scott Glenn's, Wes, for the affections of Sissy. At the time the film was made, Gilley's was the largest nightclub in the world in square footage, according to the *Guinness Book of World Records*. Sissy is cast as a spunky young woman who learns to ride the bulls herself.

John Travolta had a mechanical bull installed in his home two months before production began and became so good that he was allowed to dismiss the stunt double and do the bull riding takes himself. Like the film's star, Winger and Glenn braved the threat of spinal injury by mastering the technique so well that they were also able to do their own stunt work. In order to place the cameras properly,

Mechanical bull

the mattresses that usually surrounded the bull to cushion falls were removed.

DID YOU  KNOW?

Mechanical bulls were originally created to help bronc and bull riders train for rodeo events. The use of the device as a form of entertainment was popularized by Gilley's nightclub owner Sherwood Cryer.

The Music

The soundtrack album from the movie was a major hit and sold several million copies. One of the songs, "Looking for Love," by American country singer Johnny Lee, probably best describes the movie's plot. The film also features the hit tunes "Stand by Me," "Could I Have This Dance?" and "All Night Long."

Urban Cowboys

"Urban" means belonging or relating to a town or city, and an "urban cowboy" is a city person that dresses in western-style clothes. The "urban cowboy" catchphrase gained popularity following 1980 release of the movie *Urban Cowboy*. The film sparked a renaissance of sorts in cowboy fashion and country and western music.

THE BEST OF THE 1950s AND '60s

Westerns were by far the most popular genre of television show in the 1950s and '60s, when several hundred were aired. There have been literally hundreds of great cowboy TV series over the years, and some of the more popular ones had very long runs, indeed. The most popular series all had outstanding casts and featured action and justice. Endings were generally fairly predictable, with the good guy prevailing over the villain. Some of the best and longest running TV series are listed in chronological order in this chapter.

Hopalong Cassidy (1949–54)

Hopalong Cassidy was *the* original network western television series and first aired on June 24, 1949. It set the stage for upcoming TV series by portraying the cowboy as a genuine hero. Hopalong Cassidy was a fictional cowboy hero created in 1904 by author Clarence E. Mulford, whose popular short stories and novels based on the character later evolved into both television and radio series. Although Mulford's original character was rude, dangerous and rough talking, he was transformed into a clean-cut American cowboy hero for television. Nicknamed "Hoppy," he rode a white horse called Topper and usually dressed in black cowboy clothes with a black cowboy hat, an exception to the long-standing western film stereotype that only villains wore black hats. The TV plots were pretty basic: Hopalong and his horse Topper would catch bad guys, along with sidekick character Red Connors for comic relief.

DID YOU  KNOW?

Louis L'Amour wrote four novels featuring Hopalong Cassidy, and all of them are still in print.

The Life and Legend of Wyatt Earp (1955–61)

The Life and Legend of Wyatt Earp was a biographical series loosely based on the life of famous frontier marshal Wyatt Earp and featured actor Hugh O'Brian in the title role. The half-hour, black-and-white program aired for 229 episodes on ABC. In the series, Marshal Earp keeps the law, first in Kansas (three seasons) and later in Arizona.

DID YOU  KNOW?

In the show, Marshal Earp carried a Buntline Special, a pistol with a 12-inch barrel, though there is no factual evidence that Wyatt Earp ever owned such a gun. The Colt Buntline Special is a variant of the long-barreled Colt Single Action Army revolver. Toy replicas of the weapon became popular during the period the series was originally broadcast.

AWESOME

Despite leading a very dangerous lifestyle, the real Wyatt Earp lived to be 81 years old. He was born in 1848 and died in 1929.

Gunsmoke (1955–75)

Marshal Matt Dillon, played by James Arness, was the main character in the series *Gunsmoke*. He was responsible for keeping the peace in rough-and-tumble Dodge City during the settlement of the American West. Other actors in the series included Dennis Weaver as Chester Goode, Matt's sidekick; Milburn Stone as Dr. G. "Doc" Adams (later Galen "Doc" Adams), the town physician; Amanda Blake as Miss Kitty Russell, the saloonkeeper; and Ken Curtis as Festus Hagen, Matt's deputy. Although Marshal Dillon and Miss Kitty clearly had a close personal relationship, the two never married. Arness and Stone remained with the show for its entire run, though Stone missed seven episodes in 1971. This show, along with *The Life and Legend of Wyatt Earp*, helped launch the great era of the TV western. Westerns became so popular on TV that by the late 1950s, there were as many as 40 series airing in prime time.

DID YOU  KNOW?

Gunsmoke was the longest-running dramatic series in network history until NBC's *Law & Order* tied it in 2010. *Gunsmoke* ran from September 10, 1955, to March 31, 1975, on CBS, with 635 total episodes. James Arness' 20-year prime-time run as the marshal of Dodge City was tied only in recent times by Kelsey Grammer's 20 years as Frasier Crane from 1984 to 2004 on *Cheers* and then on *Frasier*. In 1987, some actors from the original *Gunsmoke* series (James Arness, Amanda Blake, Buck Taylor and Fran Ryan) reunited for the TV movie, *Gunsmoke: Return to Dodge*, which was filmed in Alberta, Canada.

Zorro (1957–59)

Zorro was an American action-adventure drama series produced by Walt Disney Productions. Based on the well-known Zorro character (played by Guy Williams), the series premiered on October 10, 1957, on ABC. In the series, Don Diego de la Vega is recalled by his father from Spain to his home outside El Pueblo de Nuestra Señora Reina de los Ángeles sobre El Rio Porciuncula (later shortened to Los Angeles) to fight the corrupt Captain Monasterio and the other tyrants of Spanish California as the masked swordsman, Zorro. He is every bit the hero, as was the also-masked Lone Ranger in his day in a parallel series. The final network broadcast was July 2, 1959.

DID YOU KNOW?

Although *Zorro* was the most popular show in its Thursday network evening slot, the series was pulled in 1959 because of legal wrangling between Disney Studios and the ABC network.

Maverick (1957–62)

Created by Roy Huggins, *Maverick* was a western television series with comedic overtones. The show starred James Garner as Bret Maverick, a fast-talking cardsharp, and ran from September 22, 1957, to July 8, 1962, on ABC. Partway into the first season, Garner was joined by actor Jack Kelly in the role of Bart Maverick, Bret's brother. From that point on, Garner and Kelly alternated leads from week to week, sometimes teaming up for the occasional two-brother episode. The Mavericks were Texas poker players who traveled all over the Old West and on Mississippi riverboats, constantly getting into dangerous situations that typically involved money or women or both. The series featured a catchy theme song, which aptly characterized the legendary Old West.

DID YOU KNOW?

Jack Kelly's role as Bart Maverick was originally supposed to be just a one-shot deal, but when the producers saw the great chemistry he had with James Garner, they made him a regular. Kelly was the only *Maverick* star to appear in all five seasons of the series.

Have Gun—Will Travel (1957–63)

Have Gun—Will Travel aired on CBS from 1957 through 1963 and was third or fourth in the Nielsen ratings every year of its first four seasons. The series followed the adventures of Paladin, a gentlemanly gunfighter played by Richard Boone on TV and by John Dehner in the radio series. (The name Paladin means "vigilante protector.") Paladin generally prefers to settle matters without violence, but when forced, he is a good fighter and an excellent shot. His home base is suite 205 in the posh Hotel Carlton in San Francisco. After being hired as a mercenary, Paladin dons black trail clothing, playing the role of a "black knight," so to speak. His arsenal consists of a finely crafted revolver, a derringer hidden under his black leather gun belt and, on occasion, a custom rifle bearing a knight's head on the stock.

DID YOU KNOW?

Have Gun—Will Travel was one of the few television shows to spawn a successful radio version, which debuted on November 23, 1958. In filling out Paladin's background story in the early episodes, it's mentioned that he was a West Point graduate and a former professional soldier before the Civil War. Paladin never mentions directly which side he was on during the war.

Wagon Train (1957–65)

The series *Wagon Train* ran on the NBC network from 1957 to 1962, and then on ABC from 1962 to 1965. The show debuted at number 15 in the Nielsen ratings, rose to second place in the next three seasons, and then peaked at number one in the 1961–62 television season. After moving to ABC in the autumn of 1962, the series' ratings began to decline, and *Wagon Train* did not again make the top 20 listing.

The show chronicles the adventures of a wagon train making its way from post–Civil War Missouri to California through the Great Plains, deserts and Rocky Mountains. Ward Bond originated the character of Major Seth Adams, the gruff wagon master, but upon his death was replaced by John McIntire, with actor Robert Horton as the scout. Both Bond and Horton were very popular TV stars in their day, and Bond made 23 movies with John Wayne.

DID YOU KNOW?

A folk legend has developed that country singer Johnny Horton died in a car accident while driving to see Ward Bond at a hotel in Dallas to discuss a possible role in the fourth season of *Wagon Train*. The facts are that although Horton was killed in a car crash at 1:30 AM on November 5, 1960, and Bond died from a massive heart attack at noon that same day, the two events were unrelated. Bond was replaced by John McIntire as the wagon master in the series, but no explanation was ever given on the show for the casting change.

Wanted: Dead or Alive (1958–61)

Wanted: Dead or Alive starred Steve McQueen as soft-hearted bounty hunter Josh Randall. Randall, a Confederate veteran, carries a shortened Winchester Model 1892, called a Mare's Leg, in a holster patterned after typical gunslinger rigs that were then popular in movies and television. Though short-lived, the series launched McQueen's acting career, typically as a hero in dramatic, action-oriented movies. He later turned down roles in *Butch Cassidy and the Sundance Kid*, *Dirty Harry* and *Ocean's Eleven*.

DID YOU  KNOW?

Steve McQueen was best known for his tough-guy roles. His nickname was the "King of Cool." He died of a heart attack in Mexico at the age of 50 on November 7, 1980.

The Rifleman (1958–63)

Set in the 1880s, in the town of North Fork, New Mexico Territory, *The Rifleman* starred Chuck Connors as widowed rancher Lucas McCain and Johnny Crawford as his son, Mark. It was one of the first prime-time series to feature a widowed parent raising a child. The series featured the adventures of a rancher in the Old West who wields a customized, rapid-firing Winchester rifle—McCain could fire a round with his specially modified Winchester in three-tenths of a second. The highly popular show's half-hour episodes were filmed in black and white and aired on the ABC network from September 30, 1958, to April 8, 1963.

DID YOU  KNOW?

Chuck Connors' career included playing professional baseball for the Chicago Cubs and the Montreal Royals, as well as for the Los Angeles Angels. He was also a Boston Celtic in the first year of the Professional Basketball Association and had the dubious distinction of being the first player to shatter a glass backboard. At 6 feet 5 inches, he cut an impressive figure. Despite playing numerous other roles, Connors found himself typecast as the Rifleman. He died of lung cancer at age 71 in Los Angeles in 1992.

Rawhide (1959–65)

Rawhide starred regular cast members Eric Fleming as trail boss Gil Favor and Clint Eastwood as ramrod (and trail boss in season eight) Rowdy Yates, with Paul Brinegar as George Washington Wishbone, the cantankerous cook. Literally dozens of notable guests appeared in the series. Set in the 1860s, *Rawhide* portrays the challenges faced by the men on a cattle drive that begins in San Antonio, Texas, and makes its way along the Sedalia Trail to Missouri. In later seasons, Favor and his crew push the cattle up the newer Chisum Trail from Paris, Texas, to New Mexico. The series aired for eight seasons on the CBS network on Friday nights, from January 9, 1959, to September 3, 1965, before moving to Tuesday nights from September 14, 1965, until January 4, 1966, with a total of 217 episodes.

Sedalia Stats

In the TV series, the Sedalia Trail (also known as the Shawnee Trail) ran from San Antonio, Texas, to Sedalia, Missouri, a distance of approximately 720 miles (1158 kilometers). In an average day, the cattle may have traveled a distance of only 8 miles (13 kilometers), so the entire cattle drive on the Sedalia Trail would have taken about 90 days.

DID YOU KNOW?

Spanning seven and a half years, *Rawhide* was the fifth longest running television western, exceeded only by eight years of *Wagon Train*, nine years of *The Virginian*, 14 years of *Bonanza* and 20 years of *Gunsmoke*. Drovers on the show were paid a dollar a day and fed all they could eat.

Lorne Greene as Ben Cartwright

Bonanza (1959–73)

The popular NBC television series *Bonanza* featured the Cartwright family and was set on the sweeping Ponderosa

Ranch, located south of Virginia City, Nevada, along Lake Tahoe. The show chronicled the lives and adventures of patriarch Ben and his three sons. It starred legendary Canadian actor Lorne Greene as Ben Cartwright, Pernell Roberts as Adam Cartwright, Dan Blocker as Eric "Hoss" Cartwright, Michael Landon as "Little" Joe Cartwright and, in later seasons, David Canary as Candy Canaday. Two years after Pernell Roberts left *Bonanza*, Canaday was brought in as a new character to fill the gap and add some more "spark" to the already popular series. David Canary was perfectly cast as "Candy" Canaday, the honorary foreman of the Ponderosa Ranch.

Each episode famously opened with a blazing map of the Ponderosa Ranch and the Cartwright family on horseback. The series' catchy theme song remains one of television's most memorable.

Bonanza ran from September 12, 1959, to January 16, 1973, in prime time on Sunday evenings. Lasting 14 seasons and 430 episodes, it ranks as the second longest running western series (behind *Gunsmoke*) and continues to air in syndication.

DID YOU  KNOW?

Dan Blocker, who played the likeable Eric "Hoss" Cartwright, was a Korean War veteran. On May 13, 1972, Blocker died in Los Angeles of a pulmonary embolism following gallbladder surgery. The writers of *Bonanza* took the unusual step of referencing a major character's death in the show's storyline that autumn. The series lasted another season without Hoss—the 14th and final season ended nine episodes shy of a full season on January 16, 1973.

The Virginian (1962–71)

The Virginian (known as *The Men From Shiloh* in its final year) aired on NBC from 1962 to 1971 for a total of 249 episodes and starred James Drury and Doug McClure. When the popular hour-long series *Wagon Train* moved from the NBC network to ABC, *The Virginian* was proposed to replace it. Filmed in color, *The Virginian* became television's first 90-minute western series. Immensely successful, it ran for nine seasons, making it television's third longest running western.

Set in the Wyoming Territory around the 1890s and loosely based on the 1902 novel by Owen Wister, the series revolves around the tough foreman of the Shiloh Ranch, played by Drury. McClure played the character of Trampas, a rowdy cowhand who eventually settles down on the ranch.

DID YOU  KNOW?

The real name of James Drury's character, the Virginian, is never revealed and little about his past is actually made known in the course of the series.

EQUESTRIAN EXPLORERS AND LONG-DISTANCE TRAVELERS

The Long Riders' Guild is the world's first international association of equestrian explorers and long-distance travelers. Although guild officials do not consider themselves "cowboys," there are members with a cowboy history.

Exploring the World on Horseback

With members in 45 countries, every major equestrian explorer alive today belongs to the guild, including Hadji Shamsuddin of Afghanistan, who recently rode 1000 miles (1609 kilometers) through that war-zone; Jean-Louis Gouraud of France, who rode 3000 miles (4828 kilometers) from Paris to Moscow; Claudia Gottet of Switzerland, who rode 8000 miles (1287 kilometers) from the Middle East to the Alps; Adnan Azzam of Syria, who rode 10,000 miles (16,093 kilometers) from Madrid to Mecca; and Vladimir Fissenko of Russia, who rode 19,000 miles (30,578 kilometers) from Patagonia to Alaska.

Royal Geographical Society Connection

More than 100 of these extraordinary Long Riders are also Fellows of the Royal Geographical Society, including the following:

 Stephen McCutcheon of England, who is currently riding 10,000 miles (16,093 kilometers) solo from Delhi to Peking

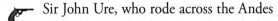 Sir John Ure, who rode across the Andes

Pedro Luiz de Aguiar of Brazil, who at the age of 70 made an 18,000-mile (28,969-kilometer) journey across Latin America

Capital Tour

Some of the historical Long Riders had their roots in the American West. George Beck, for example, rode 20,352 miles (32,753 kilometers) to all 48 state capitals in 1912.

Becoming a Member

To become a member of the Long Rider's Guild, a person must meet a number of criteria, the key being the completion of a continuous ride of at least 1000 miles (1609 kilometers). An invitation to the guild is issued at the end of the trip.

DID YOU  KNOW?

The Long Riders' Guild, established in 1994, has its headquarters in in Geneva, Switzerland. Their motto is "On the road...again and again...always!" The guild's logo is a striking image of Count Pompeii—the flying horse mascot of the Long Riders' Guild.

THROUGH TOWNS AND TIME

Alberta's Cowboy Trail takes you on a journey through the heart of Canada's Old West, home to many of the country's top rodeo stars. You can spend several days exploring this route, which covers 456 miles (735 kilometers). You might want to stop in Longview at Canadian country music legend Ian Tyson's Navajo Mug for some homemade pie. The town also features the famous Longview Jerky shop. Farther north, the main street of Cochrane is popular for its old-fashioned storefronts, shops and cafés, and the town is famous for MacKay's ice cream.

Traveling the Trail

Alberta's Cowboy Trail is a scenic road that snakes its way along the picturesque foothills of southwestern Alberta. It begins in Cardston and heads west along Highway 5 to the Waterton Lakes area, then north on Highway 6 through the agricultural community of Pincher Creek. The Trail turns west at

Sign along the Cowboy Trail

Highway 3 (the Crowsnest Highway), then meets Highway 22, the official Cowboy Trail, just past Lundbreck. It continues north through Longview, Black Diamond, Turner Valley and Millarville, passing through some of the province's historic and iconic ranchlands.

The highway jogs west at Highway 22X, and about 18 miles (30 kilometers) later, it turns north again and passes through the hamlet of Bragg Creek, where Highway 22X ends. Highway 22 continues north past the Trans-Canada Highway (Highway 1) west of Calgary, through the town of Cochrane and the village of Cremona to Highway 27.

The Trail continues generally northward through Sundre, Caroline, Rocky Mountain House and Drayton Valley until it intersects Highway 16 (Yellowhead Highway) at Entwistle, approximately 53 miles (85 kilometers) west of Edmonton.

After briefly turning west for 4 miles (6 kilometers), it continues north to cross Highway 43 at Mayerthorpe, where it terminates 5 miles (8 kilometers) north of the town at Highway 18.

Bar U Ranch National Historic Site

Just west of the junction of Highway 22 and Highway 540 is the Bar U Ranch National Historic Site. Established in 1882, the ranch was visited by the likes of HRH Prince Edward of Wales and Harry Alonzo Longabaugh, the real Sundance Kid. You can take a folksy horse-drawn wagon ride and tour the ranch, which stands in tribute to the ranching history of western Canada.

Trail Tourism

The Cowboy Trail Tourism Association provides information about the Cowboy Trail. You can find their website at www.thecowboytrail.com. There's also a very informative book written by D. Larraine Andrews called *The Cowboy Trail: A Guide to Alberta's Historic Cowboy Country* (2006).

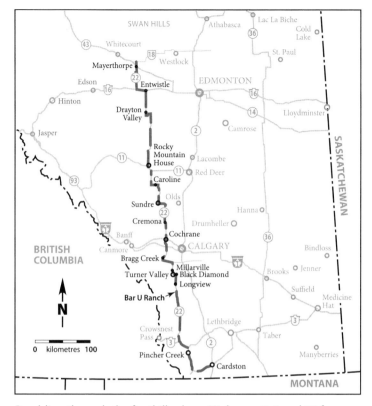

Rambling through the foothills along Highways 5, 6 and 22 from Cardston to Mayerthorpe, the Cowby Trail highlights Alberta's cowboy heritage.

The American Cowboy Trail

There is also a Cowboy Trail in Nebraska. It covers 321 miles (571 kilometers) from Chadron to Norfolk and follows the old Chicago and Northwestern rail route. You can hike, bike or horseback ride a total of 195 miles (314 kilometers) on completed trail from Norfolk to Valentine.

LARGER THAN LIFE

Pecos Bill

Pecos Bill is a fictional American cowboy who "tamed the Wild West." He was a late addition to the "big man" genre of characters, which includes American folk heroes such as Paul Bunyan and John Henry. Pecos Bill was written up as a cowboy hero with superhuman abilities—the embodiment of the superlatives "strongest," "meanest" and "greatest." He supposedly invented calf roping, cattle branding and the six-shooter.

According to legend, Pecos Bill was born in Texas in the 1830s. As the story goes, he was traveling in a covered wagon as a child when he fell out, unbeknownst to the rest of his family, near the Pecos River, hence his nickname "Pecos." He was adopted and raised by a pack of coyotes before being found by his brother years later. His brother eventually persuaded Bill that he was not actually a coyote. (Remember, this is a legend and unauthenticated!) He grew up to be a cowboy and was said to have used a rattlesnake by the name of Shake as a lasso and another snake as a horsewhip. The name of his horse was Widow-Maker, though it was sometimes called Lightning, apparently because nobody else could ride him except Pecos Bill. Mind you, it was said that he also rode a mountain lion on occasion rather than a horse. His favorite food was said to be dynamite, and in the stories, Pecos Bill once even managed to lasso a tornado.

DID YOU KNOW?

Pecos Bill was initially popularized by author Edward O'Reilly in 1916. The stories are of very doubtful authenticity, immortalized in numerous tall tales of the Old West during the settlement of the American Southwest. They began as short stories by O'Reilly and were first published in *The Century* magazine, and then later collected and reprinted in a book entitled *Saga of Pecos Bill* (1923). Considered an example of "fakelore," other authors have added their own tales and created their own versions of the Pecos Bill stories over the years.

Johnny Chinook

Johnny Chinook was a legendary Métis cowboy and rancher of the Canadian West. Folk hero Johnny's tall tales were set in Alberta's wild western years. He allegedly spent his life traveling around the province doing all sorts of jobs and having all sorts of adventures. Johnny is joined by some other memorable characters from Alberta's history as part of the folklore. The book entitled *Johnny Chinook: Tall Tales and True from the Canadian West* (1967) was written by Robert E. Gard and chronicles Johnny's exploits.

DID YOU KNOW?

Johnny always wears red socks, which is odd nowadays and for the time period in which he supposedly lived.

ALBERTA ATTRACTIONS

Travel Alberta

The Travel Alberta website (www.travelalberta.com) provides an outline of some of the guest ranches in Alberta. The Alberta Western & Cowboy Vacations Association website (www.albertacountryvacation.com) is another great source of information about Alberta's trail rides, cattle drives, guest and working ranches and country vacations, which are too numerous to list in this book. Alberta is a veritable hotbed of guest ranches and also offers many outstanding trail rides, especially in the Rockies. If you've never been on a weeklong trail ride, you should put this on your bucket list because it's one of the finest vacations you'll likely ever experience. You'll also have the opportunity to sample some of Canada's best in western cuisine on Alberta's guest ranches.

A Few to Sample

Some guest ranches are small, like the Black Cat Guest Ranch, which is located just outside Jasper National Park. Established in 1935, it is one of Alberta's oldest and has been under the present ownership since 1970. Other guest ranches such as the Rafter Six Ranch near Banff National Park are actually country resorts that feature a host of riding and outdoor experiences, along with unique western cuisine and dining experiences.

A little dude

DID YOU  KNOW?

Alberta has lots of guest ranches that provide winter ranch experiences, from sleigh rides to winter riding adventures to overnight cabin stays.

BEAUTIFUL BRITISH COLUMBIA

BC Tourist Ranch Resources

There are many guest ranches in British Columbia, and the BC Guest Ranchers' Association (bcguestranches.com) offers a diverse selection of the incredible variety of ranch experiences that the province has to offer. British Columbia's guest and dude ranches provide the opportunity to ride horses and relax and enjoy nature at the same destination. The Destination BC website (www.hellobc.com) features some of the guest/dude ranches and horseback riding available in BC. The British Columbia Dude Ranchers' Association website (www.duderanch.org/british-columbia-dude-ranch) is another excellent resource for information on dude ranches in the province.

Kamloops

Kamloops is a veritable hotbed of guest ranches, and under the "Ranch Experiences" category on their website, Tourism Kamloops (tourismkamloops.com) provides contact information for ranches in the area.

Quilchena Resort

Quilchena Resort, BC's destination for turn-of-the-20th-century romance, is celebrating over 100 years of business in the Nicola Valley. Established in 1908, the resort offers a relaxing stay in cattle country with an Edwardian-like dining room, authentic western saloon, coffee shop, banquet room, 15 unique rooms and a ranch house.

Trail ride

Three Bars Ranch

The Three Bars Ranch is a family-run guest ranch located in the Rocky Mountains near Cranbrook, between Banff and Glacier National Parks. It offers a plethora of outdoor adventures in addition to featuring riding experiences. This special part of the world is noted for an abundance of nature, clean, fast-moving rivers, green fields and breath-taking mountain vistas.

AWESOME

The Three Bars Ranch was voted Canada's number one guest ranch in 2009 and 2010, and Canada's Best Family Ranch in 2011.

Bull River Guest Ranch

The Bull River Guest Ranch is nestled in the foothills of the Rocky Mountains, tucked away in a quiet, picturesque part of the BC Kootenays.

Historic Hat Creek Ranch

The Historic Hat Creek Ranch in British Columbia's Cariboo region north of Cache Creek dates back to the 1870s. It offers a rare opportunity to explore the original buildings of a key location in the transportation history of the Cariboo. The ranch offers stagecoach rides along the historic Cariboo Wagon Road, gold panning, archery and more.

SASKATCHEWAN SIGHTS

Sturgeon River Ranch

The Sturgeon River Ranch is located on the west side of Prince Albert National Park. The ranch features horseback rides, which include searching for the wild bison herd in the park (it's the largest free-ranging plains bison herd in Canada), and overnight stays in tipis and covered wagons.

Historic Reesor Ranch

The Historic Reesor Ranch is located in the southwest corner of Saskatchewan near Cypress Hills Interprovincial Park. The ranch has been in the family for 109 years. Owner Scott Reesor is also a cowboy poet.

La Reata Ranch

The La Reata Ranch is run by German-born George Gaber. A working cattle ranch, it sits along the shore of Lake Diefenbaker between the town of Kyle and the city of Swift Current and features over 5000 acres (2023 hectares) of rolling native grasslands.

Beaver Creek Ranch

The Beaver Creek Ranch is located north of Regina, in the Qu'Appelle Valley near Lumsden. Owned by the Clemens family, this working ranch provides a great cowboy experience that also features western cowboy cookouts, with buffalo or beef steaks and hamburgers with all the fixings.

THE AMERICAN WEST

An evening around the campfire

Big Ranches in the Grand Canyon State

Arizona, the Grand Canyon State, has a host of dude ranches featured online at the Arizona Guide website (www.arizonaguide.com/hotels-lodging/guest-ranches). One of the most impressive attractions of guest ranches in Arizona is their huge size—up to 60,000 acres (24,281 hectares)—and their longevity.

DID YOU KNOW?

Tanque Verde Ranch is one of America's best old-time cattle and guest ranches. The Tanque Verde Ranch Resort was named Best Dude Ranch in Arizona by *Arizona Republic* newspaper in 2012, as well as a Top Ten Family Resort by the Travel Channel since 2007 and a Top Five Ranch by *Condé Nast Traveler* in 2008. It also won a silver award for Outstanding Southwestern Cuisine from *Tucson Lifestyle* magazine in 2013.

Colorful Colorado

The Colorado Dude & Guest Ranch Association website (www.coloradoranch.com) features many ranch vacations. Nicknamed the Centennial State, Colorado is noted for its picturesque landscape of mountains, plains, mesas and canyons; however, it's perhaps best known for its traditional western cowboy culture and agricultural ranching lifestyle. Colorado dude ranches offer great hospitality and western horseback riding year-round. Ranch vacations also offer the opportunity to visit one of three spectacular national parks in the state while on a horse-riding holiday, as well as Native American ruins and remnant ghost towns from the days of the 1858–61 gold rush.

Magnificent Montana

Dude ranches in Montana are featured on the Montana Dude Ranchers' Association website (www.montanadra.com) and run the gamut of western vacations. Many are authentic working ranches where you can get involved in real working-ranch activities such as moving cattle and fixing fences, and even have a go at natural horsemanship training if the guest ranch has a horse breeding and training program.

Wild Wyoming

The picturesque Wyoming landscape is a big draw for people, and Wyoming dude ranches offer a wide range of exciting opportunities and western cuisine for all ages. On the "age" note—this should not be a barrier for anyone interested in horseback riding, which can be enjoyed by people of all ages. The Dude Ranchers' Association website (www.duderanch. org/wyoming-dude-ranch) bills the state as being "True cowboy country, with few people and vast, open spaces. It is a land that inspires dreams of riding horseback across the plains"—not a surprising testimonial coming from the Cowboy State.

Texas Tourism

Not surprisingly, Texas is huge on dude ranches, and the state markets all sorts of vacation packages from "cowgirl specials" to "year-round children's specials." Bandera, in Texas Hill Country, is the epicenter of the dude ranch industry in the state, and some Bandera-area ranches date back to the 1890s. The ranches feature all kinds of vacation opportunities, including upland bird hunting and, of course, good 'ol Texas cuisine.

THE LITERARY COWBOY

Western novels have inspired readers largely because of authors such as Zane Grey, Will James, Louis L'Amour and Elmer Kelton.

The Western Fiction Novel

The western fiction novel in American literature had its genesis with tales of the frontier, and the most famous of the early 19th-century frontier authors was James Fenimore Cooper, author of *The Last of the Mohicans*. Western fiction is a genre of literature set in the frontier of the American Old West, typically from the late 18th to the late 19th century. Well-known writers of the genre include Zane Grey in the early 1900s and Louis L'Amour in the mid 20th century. The western genre peaked in the early 1960s, largely owing to the immense popularity of television series such as *Gunsmoke* and *Bonanza*, though there were numerous other popular western TV series at the time. The drop in popularity in these series in the late 1960s probably had an effect on western literature, and interest in the genre began to wane. Readership began to drop off in the mid- to late 1970s and has reached a new low in the 2000s.

DID YOU  KNOW?

Western authors are represented by the Western Writers of America, who present the annual Spur Awards and the Owen Wister Award for Lifetime Achievement. The organization was founded in 1953 to promote the literature of the American West.

WESTERN AUTHORS

Will James (1892–1942)

Will James was one of Canada's best-known cowboy authors and artists. Born Joseph Ernest Nephtali Dufault in 1892 in Saint-Nazaire-d'Acton, Quebec, he later settled near Val Marie, Saskatchewan, in 1910. He was taught wrangling by local cowboy Pierre Beaupre, and the two built separate homesteads along the Frenchman River in southwestern Saskatchewan. In 1913, he moved to the United States with a new name—William Roderick James. He served time in a Nevada prison for rustling cattle and worked on ranches in several western states before finally settling in California and re-inventing himself as an artist and author.

In his book *Ride for the High Points: The Real Story of Will James* (1987), author Jim Bramlett recounts James' all-too-brief career as a celebrated and admired icon of the West, which ended in 1942 after a long bout with alcoholism. James wrote 27 cowboy books during his writing career; his first, *Cowboys North and South,* was published in 1924.

DID YOU  KNOW?

In 1988, the National Film Board of Canada sponsored an 83-minute biography entitled *Alias Will James*, which commemorates the French Canadian's life and features his art and story craft. Canadian country and western singer Ian Tyson wrote "The Man They Called Will James" for the film score. Sadly, James' life was much like the song's lyrics, "If whiskey was his mistress, Then his true love was the West," because he died an alcoholic.

COWBOY WISDOM

"Whiskey—the reason I wake up every afternoon."

Zane Grey at the University of Pennsylvania, 1895

Zane Grey (1872–1939)

Zane Grey was born in Zanesville, Ohio. He wrote over 90 books, and his bestseller, *Riders of the Purple Sage* (1912), also probably his best-known novel, is considered the most popular western novel of all time by some. Grey wrote not only westerns, but also two hunting books, six children's books, three baseball books and eight fishing books. A successful author, Grey had the time and money to engage in his first and greatest passion, sport fishing. From 1918 until 1932, he was a regular contributor to *Outdoor Life* magazine, and as one of the magazine's first celebrity writers, he popularized big-game fishing based on his worldwide fishing adventures. Grey fished out of Wedgeport, Nova Scotia, for many summers and set a world record for the largest bluefin tuna on August 24, 1924, when he caught one weighing 758 pounds (343 kilograms).

DID YOU  **KNOW?**

As of 2012, Zane Grey's novels and short stories have been the subject of 112 films, two television episodes and a TV series, *Dick Powell's Zane Grey Theater*. His total book sales exceed 40 million copies.

Louis L'Amour (1908–1988)

Louis L'Amour was born Louis Dearborn LaMoore in Jamestown, North Dakota. It was his first western novel, *Hondo*, published in 1953, that gained him instant success as a writer. Although L'Amour later wrote works in different genres, it was his many westerns that brought him great popularity among readers. His top-rated titles include *Last of the Breed*, *The Walking Drum*, *Sackett's Land*, *Hondo* and *The Lonesome Gods*. At the time of his death, all 101 of his works were in still print (89 novels, 14 short-story collections and one full-length work of nonfiction), and he was considered one of the world's most popular writers.

DID YOU KNOW?

L'Amour's total sales have surpassed those of every other author of western fiction in the history of the genre. By 2010, his book sales had exceeded 320 million copies. More than 45 of his novels have been adapted into Hollywood films.

Elmer Kelton, 2007

Elmer Kelton (1926–2009)

Bestselling author of more than 40 western novels, Texas-born Elmer Kelton was mostly noted for his novels *The Good Old Boys* and *The Time It Never Rained*. He was voted the

Best Western Writer of All Time by the Western Writers of America. In 1995, *The Good Old Boys* was made into a Turner Network Television film of the same name, starring Tommy Lee Jones. Eight Kelton novels, *Buffalo Wagons*, *The Day the Cowboys Quit*, *The Time It Never Rained*, *Eyes of the Hawk*, *Slaughter*, *The Far Canyon*, *Many a River* and *The Way of the Coyote*, have won Spur Awards from the Western Writers of America.

DID YOU  KNOW?

A life-size statue of Elmer Kelton can be found at the Stephens Central Library in San Angelo, Texas.

COWBOY MAGAZINES

Although there has been a downturn in the number of western novels of late, cowboy magazines are alive and well despite claims that cowboys might perhaps be a thing of the past.

Canadian Cowboy Country

Founded in 1997, the Edmonton-based *Canadian Cowboy Country* magazine is published six times a year by Rob Tanner. The magazine's website bills it as being "Dedicated to the preservation of western heritage and celebrates Canada's unique cowboy culture. In each issue, readers ride into the heart of the Canadian West and immerse themselves with the people and places that define this unique western lifestyle." Interestingly, the magazine profiles being a cowboy as "a state of mind."

Western Horse Review

Based out of Calgary, Alberta, *Western Horse Review* magazine is published six times a year and focuses on horsemanship and cowboy culture, while also featuring articles on western lifestyle. Their website claims, "The voice of the Canadian western rider is represented in every issue of *Western Horse Review.* This is our great Canadian western world and we celebrate it—in all facets of the western lifestyle—from country living, horse ownership, competition, recreational riding, vacations, home decorating and fashion."

American Cowboy

American Cowboy magazine, published bi-monthly, is billed as being "Devoted to the spirit, look and style of the West." According to Facebook, "*American Cowboy* is the cultural chronicler of the West, covering history and heritage, travel and events, art and entertainment, food and fashion." The magazine also features a monthly newsletter. Many Hollywood western movie stars such as John Wayne and Clint Eastwood have graced the covers of this publication.

Cosmic Cowgirls

Cosmic Cowgirls magazine lays claim to being "a place where the poets, the artists, the thinkers, the dreamers, the revolutionaries, the knitters, the wild and the holy ones come together to share a cup of virtual tea and tell our stories. *Cosmic Cowgirls* magazine is a department of Cosmic Cowgirls, LLC [Limited Liability Corporation], a woman and girl owned publishing and production house and school that turns lives into legends!" The magazine is based out of Healdsburg, California, and publishes twice a week (104 issues per year). It started publishing in November 2010.

Cowboys & Indians

Cowboys & Indians magazine covers western life and style, art and entertainment, and travel and adventure, as well as food and wine. The magazine was established in 1993 and is published out of Dallas, Texas. According to their website: "An international magazine of the highest quality, *Cowboys & Indians* encompasses everything exceptional about the American West: history and legend, hardworking people, dramatic vistas, enduring values." Primarily a lifestyle magazine, *Cowboys & Indians* is designed to appeal to a broad audience.

Cowgirl

Cowgirl is a bi-monthly magazine that features decidedly feminine, trendy content with the following website billing: "Featuring the best of the modern west including stylish accessories for horse and home, hot fashion, luxurious dream getaways, western design trends and expert equestrian advice to inspire, educate and entertain the modern cowgirl!" The magazine is published out of Cave Creek, Arizona, and also features an e-newsletter.

Cowgirls In Style

Published four times a year, *Cowgirls In Style* boldly claims to be "The magazine with Cowgirl Style and a bit of Runway Flair." In introducing this magazine, editor-in-chief Susie Lynn proclaims it to be "a totally new, hip magazine to rock the Cowgirl World!!...Not only does *Cowgirls In Style* feature Cowgirl fashion, but we also feature fun Country destinations to visit for not only the family, but a romantic getaway."

Cowgirl Living

Cowgirl Living magazine was launched in 2008 as a bi-monthly, glossy publication for women who are interested in a western way of life. The publication was subtitled "A Magazine for Western Women." Their website is down and it appears that this magazine is no longer in print.

True Cowboy

According to their website, *True Cowboy* magazine "is a lifestyle magazine chock full of colorful western history and the cowboys, cowgirls and folks that made the West what it was and is today." Their stated mission is "to globally educate and raise awareness of the plight of the wild mustangs, horses and burros in the great USA and to achieve a moratorium on dangerous and fatal helicopter roundups, separation from their herd families, short- and long-term penning, inhumane slaughter and establishing the Restore Our American Mustangs Bill (ROAM) to a finite government protection act that includes, along with preservation tenets, restoring the wild ones to their natural habitat on the plentiful and bountiful plains of Western America!" The front cover of each issue features an attractive "Buckle Bunny," presumably to boost male readership.

NOTES ON SOURCES

Much of the information in this book was obtained online from various websites as noted in the text. The National Cowboy and Western Heritage Museum, San Jacinto River Authority, is credited as a source of trivia. CuChullaine O'Reilly of the Long Riders' Guild kindly responded to my request to include information about the guild in this book. Some cowboy lingo was sourced online from Western Lingo, Slang and Phrases: A Writer's Guide to the Old West. Chad MacPherson, general manager of the Saskatchewan Stock Growers Association, provided key historical information about ranches, ranching and pioneer ranchers in Saskatchewan. The Encyclopedia of Saskatchewan website was also used as a source of information about cowboys and ranching in Saskatchewan. Tourism agency staff in Alberta, British Columbia and Saskatchewan all provided considerable source information about cowboys, the history of ranching and dude ranches in their provinces.

Further Reading

Alberta 4-H 75th Anniversary Committee. *4-H Favorites: 75th Anniversary Cookbook*. 4-H Foundation of Alberta, 1992.

Adams, Ramon F. *Cowboy Lingo*. New York: Houghton Mifflin, 2000.

Alberta Beef Producers. *I Love Alberta Beef*. Victoria, BC: Touchwood Editions, 2004.

Anderson, Boyd M. *Beyond the Range: A History of the Saskatchewan Stock Growers Association*. Regina, SK: Saskatchewan Stock Growers Association, 1988.

Andrews, D. Larraine. *The Cowboy Trail: A Guide to Alberta's Historic Cowboy Trail*. Victoria, BC: Heritage House, 2006.

Bramlett, Jim. *Ride for the High Points: The Real Story of Will James*. Missoula, MT: Mountain Press, 1987.

Clement, Willie. *All Hat, No Horse: Cowboy Humor*. Edmonton, AB: Argenta Press, 2012.

Cross Bar Ranch. *Cross Bar Ranch Centennial Legacy Cookbook 1910–2012*. Kearney, NE: Morris Press Cookbooks, 2010.

Dempsey, Hugh A. *The Golden Age of the Canadian Cowboy*. Calgary, AB: Fifth House (Fitzhenry & Whiteside), 1995.

Elofson, Warren M. *Cowboys, Gentlemen & Cattle Thieves*. Montreal, QC, and Kingston, ON: McGill-Queen's University Press, 2000.

Gard, Robert E. *Johnny Chinook: Tall Tales and True from the Canadian West*. New York: Longmans, Green and Company, 1945.

Hoare, Jean. *Jean Hoare's Best Little Cookbook in the West*. Calgary, AB: Deadwood Publishing, 1983.

Macpherson, M.A. *Outlaws & Lawmen of Western Canada, Volume Two*. Victoria, BC: Heritage House, 1983.

Macpherson, M.A. *Outlaws of the Canadian West*. Edmonton, AB: Lone Pine Publishing, 2006.

Neering, Rosemary. *Wild West Women Travellers, Adventurers and Rebels*. Vancouver, BC: Whitecap Books, 2000.

Radford, Duane. *Fish & Wild Game Recipes, Volume 1*. Edmonton, AB: Sportscene Publications. 2006.

Richards, J.R., and K.I. Fung, *Atlas of Saskatchewan*. Saskatoon, SK: Modern Press, 1969.

Steber, Rick. *Cowboys (Tales of the Wild West, Vol. 4)*. Prineville, OR: Bonanza Publishing, 1988.

Steele, Phillip W. *Outlaws and Gunfighters of the Old West*. Gretna, LA: Pelican Publishing, 1998.

Websites

American Professional Rodeo Association. aprarodeo.com

The Cowboy Trail. www.thecowboytrail.com

The Encyclopedia of Saskatchewan. www.esask.uregina.ca

Legends of America: Western Lingo, Slang and Phrases: A Writer's Guide to the Old West. www.legendsofamerica.com/we-slang.html

Long Riders Guild. www.thelongridersguild.com

National Cowboy and Western Heritage Museum. www.nationalcowboymuseum.org

Rodeo Canada. www.rodeocanada.com

ABOUT THE AUTHOR

Duane S. Radford

Duane S. Radford is a multi-award-winning writer and photographer. He was born in Blairmore, Alberta, but grew up in Bellevue, both small towns in the Crowsnest Pass. It was there he first got his taste of the cowboy life at nearby ranches, riding horses, baling hay in the blistering sun, building and mending fences and doing farm chores. He holds both a BSc and an MSc from the University of Calgary, has written over 600 articles and two books, and has received several national communications awards. Duane is the past president of the Outdoor Writers of Canada and currently sits as the chairman of the board of directors for the organization. When he isn't writing or taking photographs, he spends much of his time outdoors, hunting and fly-fishing.